Cathedrals of Science

Cathedrals of Science

The Development of
Colonial Natural History
Museums during the Late
Nineteenth Century

SUSAN SHEETS-PYENSON

McGill-Queen's University Press
Kingston and Montreal

© McGill-Queen's University Press 1988
ISBN 0-7735-0655-1
Legal deposit fourth quarter 1988
Bibliothèque nationale du Québec

Printed in Canada on acid-free paper

This book has been published with the help of a grant
from the Social Science Federation of Canada, using
funds provided by the Social Sciences and Humanities
Research Council of Canada.

Canadian Cataloguing in Publication Data

Sheets-Pyenson, Susan, 1949–
    Cathedrals of science
    Includes bibliographical references and index.
    ISBN 0-7735-0655-1
    1. Natural history museums — History — 19th
    century.
    I. Title.
    QH70.A1S44 1988   069'.9508   C88-090267-1

For Lewis

Contents

Tables and Figure

Acknowledgments

It gives me great pleasure to acknowledge the assistance of those individuals and institutions which have made this book possible. Three research grants from the Canada Council and the Social Sciences and Humanities Research Council of Canada over the last decade, more properly aimed at indexing the scientific correspondence of John William Dawson, also acquainted me with Dawson's special relationship with the Redpath Museum. The generosity of administrators at Concordia University enabled me to travel to Argentina, Australia, and New Zealand, where I was able to research the museum activities of Dawson look-alikes in other cultures. I am also indebted to the staff of Concordia's Computer Centre, particularly Roger Flemming and Diane Sole, for their help in overcoming several bothersome difficulties.

Researching this book required the assistance of archivists, librarians, and museum curators all over the world. Here in Montreal, the staff of the McGill Archives under the direction of Marcel Caya has always been eager to offer their friendly, efficient assistance, no matter what the particular problem at hand. Although a number of years have gone by since I was fortunate enough to travel to Argentina, time does not dim the many kindnesses of those who made it pleasant to conduct historical research in a place that does not always encourage delving into the past. I am especially indebted to Clelia Filevich and Marcelo Montserrat, as well as to the Sociedad Científica Argentina for the use of its magnificent library. In Melbourne, the enthusiastic support of the director of the National Museum of Victoria, Tom Darragh, made working in their remarkable archives a great deal easier.

I am also deeply grateful to David Lank, David Oldroyd, and Lewis Pyenson, who all offered useful comments and criticisms on earlier drafts of this manuscript. The suggestions of three anonymous referees recruited by the Social Science Federation and McGill-Queen's University Press greatly helped in the final reworking of the manuscript. The suggestions of Molly Wolf were invaluable in taming the excesses of my prose. Nalini Johnson kindly checked the Spanish. I am honoured to acknowledge the generous support of the Social Science Federation for publication of this book.

Cathedrals of Science

Introduction

He who views only the produce of his own country may be said to inhabit a single world; while those who see and consider the productions of other climes bring many worlds in review before them. We are but on the borderland of knowledge; much remains hidden, reserved for far off generations, who will prosecute the examination of their Creator's works in remote countries, and make many discoveries for the pleasure and convenience of life. Posterity will see its increasing museums and the knowledge of divine wisdom flourish together; and at the same time antiquities and history, the natural sciences, the practical sciences of the manual arts will be enriched ...

Linnaeus, *Museum Adolphi Friderici Regis*, 1754[1]

The late nineteenth century witnessed an unprecedented explosion in the creation and expansion of natural history museums all over the world. This remarkable development has largely escaped the notice of historians who have paid more attention to the universities and learned societies that sometimes nurtured and supported museums. Those interested in the internal development of the sciences of natural history have also neglected the important role of these institutions. Yet those classifiers, compilers, and collectors who dominated natural history during the nineteenth century were responsible for the growth of the "museum movement" that became so powerful during the decades leading up to 1900.[2]

Collections of natural curiosities may be traced back to the third century BC, to Ptolemy's museum at Alexandria, or to the treasures hoarded by nobles and clerics since antiquity. It was, however, the great voyages of exploration of the sixteenth and seventeenth centuries that made collecting natural objects a reasonably common endeavour among the more privileged classes. The impetus behind these early museums was usually piety or superstition, both of which valued the rare or peculiar. Early collectors prized horns and bones which were said to come from unicorns, murderers, and giants, as well as mummies or less complete human remains. They celebrated the abnormal, the bizarre, and even the imaginary. Aesthetic considerations tended to determine the arrangement of museums, with the result that curators aligned objects in the most incongruous fashion — armadillos next to ostrich eggs.[3]

Gradually, especially as they gathered objects from new continents, Europeans recognized that nature itself offered enough diversity to delight the observer without recourse to monstrosities or fakes. Linnaeus recorded the sense of wonder evoked by the striking colours, extremes of size, and fascinating structures in the natural world as he catalogued the treasures of the royal Swedish museum in 1754.[4] Soon astonishment or surprise were seen as a stimulus for promoting a deeper knowledge of the kingdom of nature. At the same time, instructing the observer — resulting in moral improvement, according to nineteenth-century thinkers — came to overshadow amusement, the museum's previously dominant function.[5]

The new educational importance attached to museums is reflected in the fact that the eleventh edition of the *Encyclopedia Britannica* reports no fewer than 2,000 scientific museums in existence by 1910. This figure includes a remarkable variety of institutions. Municipal, provincial, or national governments supported many of them. Other museums belonged to learned societies, universities and colleges, or religious orders. Some traced their ancestry to the whims of an eccentric individual collector; others owed their birth to collections amassed by a geological survey or put together for an exposition. Some museums tried to embrace every known science, pure or applied; others had a more restricted domain, such as the natural history products of a particular area. Museums prospered in all kinds of quarters from a few showcases or rooms in a library, to an independent building constructed specifically for the purpose.

As museums were recast as educational institutions, questions of purpose, organization, and arrangement emerged as central concerns. For the first time in the history of museums, curators were compelled to develop collections in directions that answered the needs of diverse social groups. Increasingly during the nineteenth century, museums were expected to serve a middle class with more leisure, wealth, physical mobility, and educational opportunity than ever before. This newly articulate audience wanted "acceptable" activities that provided the perfect mixture of education and amusement. For these men and women, viewing the products of nature grew in appeal as industrialization and urbanization began to threaten the natural world around them.[6] Often museum curators were expected to reconcile the conflicting needs of public expectations and the requirements of a newly professional scientific elite.[7] As a result, curators frequently quibbled over seemingly minor issues of museum practice — how to display specimens and how many objects to exhibit, for example. But underlying these technical debates were more fundamental differences of opinion concerning the role of museums.

Attitudes towards all these different aspects of museums varied with local circumstances, institutional loyalties, and national allegiances. As one observer has remarked, even twentieth-century museums "are, inevitably, conditioned, in their aims, their atmosphere, their appearance and their sense of priorities by the country in which they find themselves."[8] The plans and procedures adopted by a government repository in a major city might seem to have little relevance to a small rural collection. Yet since museums, like other scientific institutions, seldom start from nothing, successful models served as inspiration and example for more modest attempts elsewhere. Personnel were sometimes imported in order to implement a particular plan or design. Within the constant international imitation and cross-fertilization of the time, concepts and innovations freely travelled the museum circuit during the decades preceding 1900.[9]

METROPOLITAN INSPIRATION:
THE BRITISH MUSEUM
(NATURAL HISTORY) AND
THE "NEW MUSEUM IDEA"

By the late nineteenth century, the spoils of empire had swollen the collections of the museum beyond the capacity of its quarters in Bloomsbury. A proposal to move across town into a grand new building coincided with the natural history curators' aspirations for greater autonomy. The opening of the new British Museum (Natural History), or Natural History Museum, in South Kensington in 1881 was timed to coincide with the beginning of the jubilee celebrating Victoria's accession to the throne. Few could fail to be impressed, even intimidated, as they passed under the soaring arches of the entrance to this, the world's most remarkable natural history museum.

A Gothic "temple to science," the museum exemplified Victorian architectural taste, seen earlier in the ornate structure built for the New Museum at Oxford. Following the Oxford model that incorporated biological symbolism into the design of the museum, the walls of the Natural History Museum displayed bas-relief representations of living and extinct species. The eclectic genius of the architect Alfred Waterhouse combined Romanesque arcades and Baroque staircases with cast-iron columns and a glass roof typical of contemporary railroad stations.

A handful of critics found the terracotta facing dingy and the high central hall empty, with adjacent side galleries like factory rooms, but most visitors were delighted with the new museum. It contained four acres of exhibition space, in addition to rooms for laboratories, workshops, and storage.[10]

It was not its dramatic building alone that placed the Natural History Museum in the first rank, but the overall quality and extent of its collections. Especially in paleontology and mineralogy, the Natural History Museum soon became the example to which every other national museum aspired. Specimens were well displayed, without the crowding that plagued so many government repositories that functioned more as storehouses. Exhibits made liberal use of descriptive labels, drawings, photographs, diagrams, and models. Museum publications also won praise from colleagues in sister institutions. Descriptive catalogues provided more information than the typical lists of museum holdings and served as definitive monographs, while a series of elementary guidebooks provided fine examples of lucid popularization. Because so many ideas had been tried, and because the staff were eager to share their experience with others, the Natural History Museum became the most important institution in the world for answering queries on museum practice.[11] One museum authority calls it quite simply the most influential of its kind.[12]

The Natural History Museum also became an arena for the discussion of various schemes for classifying and arranging natural history collections. By 1900, there, as elsewhere, the attractively simple new museum idea — the separation of study from exhibition materials — had triumphed.[13] According to its foremost exponent, the museum's director, William Henry Flower, the essence of the concept involved organizing museums around a dual purpose: research and popular education.[14]

Flower insisted that numerous specimens representing specific and (especially) varietal forms had little significance for the average visitor and belonged in a segregated study section. He compared the practice of exhibiting every museum specimen to the obviously silly procedure of framing and hanging each page in every library book. The observer who confronted row after row of objects came away, if not bewildered, at least bored. Instead, the liberal use of storage drawers and cabinets meant that specimens could be preserved from dust, pests, and light, housed in minimal space, and easily retrieved by researchers. To make the study collections truly useful, the rooms next to the exhibits where the research materials were housed needed to be furnished with adequate tables, reference books, proper lighting, and an accessible museum staff.[15] (See Figure 1.)

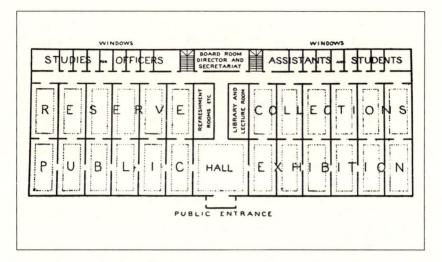

Figure 1

W.H. Flower's plan for the arrangement of an ideal natural history museum
Source: W.H. Flower, *Essays on Museums and Other Subjects Connected with Natural History* (London and New York: Macmillan & Co. 1898), 50.

The public exhibits, by contrast, were designed to give the layman a general understanding of the kingdoms of nature. Only the best specimens were to be displayed, in order to illustrate a particular principle or taxonomic category. No duplication of materials was permitted. Specimens were to be shown in uncrowded cases at a reasonable height, accompanied by informative labels. The curator might fashion his exhibits around such specific themes or concepts as geographical distribution or evolution. His resources could lead him to emphasize one group while excluding others. The function of guidebooks and catalogues was to increase the educational value of the public materials.[16]

Even before Flower's time, John Edward Gray, Keeper of Zoology during the middle decades of the nineteenth century, had tried to persuade his colleagues at the British Museum to follow a similar plan. Carefully pruned and arranged collections, he argued, gave the visitor "the greatest amount of instruction in the shortest most direct manner." Serious students, who could more easily compare and measure objects by using unmounted specimens in ordinary rooms away from onlookers, would also benefit, he insisted.[17] But these ideas threatened the designs of the formidable and influential Richard Owen, Flower's predecessor as superintendent, for a revitalized "national museum of natural history." The purpose of a national repository, Owen insisted, was to display every varietal and specific form, an aim that a lesser collection with limited resources could not hope to attain. Owen's plan called for a massive structure to accommodate the largest possible specimens of huge mammals like elephants and whales. Even duplicates could be exhibited in "distinct series with different aims," such as in separate taxonomic, educational, and "British" collections.[18]

Owen's dream seemed to be materializing as he superintended the transfer of the British Museum's natural history collections from Bloomsbury to South Kensington during the early 1880s. Yet with the move completed and Flower succeeding to the directorship in 1884, Gray's views began to enjoy a renaissance. For example, Owen's plan for synoptic displays as an index to the larger collection, which were originally to occupy "chapels" flanking the central hall, never found favour with his successors.[19] Such an abstract of the general collection became unnecessary because Flower and other curators mounted selective, not comprehensive, exhibits.

The new museum idea, ultimately triumphing at the Natural History Museum, helped to transform museum practice in other parts of the world. By 1900, most museum directors accepted the principle that "less was more" instructive in museum displays, and that the remaining inventory of specimens should be reserved for scientific investigators. Nonetheless, the adoption of the new museum idea posed a quandary that confused the efforts of curators over the next several decades. Museums were intended to serve two distinct audiences simultaneously: a few scholars and the public at large. But it was difficult, if not impossible, to respond equally to the needs of both groups. Concentrating on scientific requirements left directors open to the charge of neglecting their responsibilities to the public. Emphasizing popular education, on the other hand, suggested that museums were negligent in their research duties. The conflict between these two aims constantly vexed museum administrators everywhere.[20]

OTHER METROPOLITAN MUSEUMS:
EUROPE AND THE UNITED STATES

While the British Museum expanded and was reorganized, museums elsewhere in Europe experienced a surge of growth stimulated by the increasing size of their collections since the mid-century. Many new buildings were constructed, and there were additions and renovations to old ones. Vienna's expensive Imperial Natural History Museum opened to generous praise from "new museum" enthusiasts in 1889. In the same year, the zoological collections at the Paris Museum were moved to new Romanesque quarters decorated with animal carvings. A decade later, the anatomy and anthropolgy departments found improved accommodation. Around the same time, the Bohemian Museum opened in Prague, and in Brussels the Royal Belgian Museum inaugurated new buildings.[21]

Most continental museums displayed every object in their possession and followed what Gray had contemptuously labelled the "French plan." This called for "attaching each specimen to a separate stand, and marshalling them like soldiers on the shelves of a large open case."[22] A few museums, though, became converts to the views being articulated across the channel. The Prague museum, for example, displayed lifelike exhibits incorporating natural surroundings. It also made liberal use of drawings and models. The new building in Vienna separated exhibits from an internal core of workrooms, storage, and study collections.[23]

By 1900, Germany could claim 150 museums of natural history, Britain 250, and France 300, and the United States had a respectable 250.[24] In America, where museums had grown in numbers and improved in quality during the latter half of the nineteenth century, successful institutions traditionally depended upon individual initiative. Examples include the Museum of Comparative Zoology, for which its director, Louis Agassiz, raised $300,000, and the museum at Yale University, which benefited from the philanthropist George Peabody's bequests. Public museums directed by trustees and supported by government gradually began to supplant the cabinets of natural history typically associated with private colleges, lyceums, and academies.[25] Foremost among public institutions were the American Museum of Natural History in New York City, established in 1869, and the National Museum, part of the Smithsonian Institution, in Washington, DC. In 1877, the American Museum of Natural History moved into new quarters that occupied thirteen acres. Two years later the National Museum began to construct a new building to house the donations received upon the dismantling of the Philadelphia Exposition of 1876. The museum's functional structure attracted worldwide attention for covering more than two acres while costing taxpayers only $250,000.[26]

Like the British, the Americans had become expert at mounting explanatory and lifelike displays, incorporating model habitats, charts, diagrams, and photographs. The National Museum perfected the use of plaster casts to make fragments of bone and fossils more comprehensible, to permit the reconstruction of partial skeletons, or to fill the gaps in a series of specimens. Along with the American Museum of Natural History, it established a reputation for portraying animal groups in their natural environments. This method, initiated with birds and mammals, was soon extended to fish, invertebrates, and fossils, and finally to plants, through the use of finely worked glass and wax replicas. Both museums benefited from the techniques pioneered by Henry Ward's taxidermy firm in Rochester, NY, by hiring his trainees as curators.[27]

The man most responsible for the progressiveness of American museums was George Brown Goode, assistant secretary of the Smithsonian Institution and director of its National Museum. In one of his most famous addresses, delivered in 1895 before the British Museums Association meeting in Newcastle, Goode treated the directing of a natural history museum as an exercise to be rationalized, not unlike running a business enterprise. He formulated five "principles of museum administration." These included the necessity for competent curators, a suitable building, a stable organization, a definite plan, and good collections.[28] These rules, drawn up by Goode to be prescriptive, may be taken by historians as norms. In other words, Goode's proposals, because of their widespread applicability and general acceptance, are the ideal to which museums all over the world might be expected to aspire around 1900.[29] His ideas are especially noteworthy for supplying a theoretical overview of museum procedures and practices, and for coming, as they do, from one of the foremost representatives of the emerging class of museum professionals. We shall return to Goode's didactic views in the chapters that follow by using his principles to dictate their headings.

COLONIAL MUSEUMS:
F.A. BATHER'S SURVEY OF 1893

The advances and expansion of natural history museums in European and American cities during the latter half of the nineteenth century have been more widely appreciated than their proliferation in other parts of the world at about the same time. With the gradual accumulation of capital in the hinterland — coming from the development and exploitation of natural resources, in turn made possible by improved transportation networks — colonial legislatures began to support public museums.[30] As part of a survey conducted under the auspices of the Museums Association in 1893, British Museum curator F.A. Bather evaluated museum resources throughout the empire. What united these scattered and diverse institutions, according to Bather, was their colonial status. His paper is unique in its time for supplying cross-cultural comparisons and attempting general definitions of that little-studied category, colonial museums. Forty years would elapse before Bather's pioneering work was further elaborated and expanded in the series of directories and reports compiled by Henry A. Miers and Sydney F. Markham.

The first characteristic of a colonial museum, Bather argued, was its emphasis on local specimens. Visitors to the museum — whether newcomers from abroad or people from out of town — came to see native products, which were best kept apart from any other collections the museum might possess. In order to encourage and sustain support by residents, Bather reasoned, all donations, no matter how common, should be accepted. The other special interest of most visitors involved applied science. Although Bather pitied the curator who had to spend his days analyzing ores, an emphasis on practical matters had to be tolerated; it was better than having no publicly recognized "useful" role and hence being under constant threat of closure. If separate technological museums were established, support for natural history museums might dwindle to nothing.[31]

The second characteristic that Bather used to distinguish colonial museums was their fundamental dependence upon foreign institutions. Bather argued that external support, particularly support from the mother country, enabled colonial museums to weather day-to-day problems such as periodic financial crises, insect invasions, and deleterious climates. Help might take the form of specimen exchanges or the advice of specialists whose skills were unavailable in the colony.[32] Without the aid of metropolitan institutions, museums in the hinterland could neither properly function nor ultimately survive.

Despite the originality of Bather's approach, it is questionable whether he captured the essence of the colonial museum. Certainly curatorial staffs recognized the necessity of ministering to the needs of the local populace, whose support they required to overcome their daily tribulations. But colonial museums depended upon metropolitan museums not only for materials but also for architectural designs, organizational models, and qualified personnel. Bather's failure to discuss the actual political or economic status of the countries in question probably results from his exclusive concern with Britain's overseas possessions. The omission is significant, nevertheless, because colonialism in science need not follow the mapmakers' or diplomats' charts. Historians now recognize that new nations such as Canada and Argentina were as dependent on European traditions at the end of the nineteenth century as were *de facto* colonies like Australia and New Zealand.

Bather's major limitation, however, was to underestimate and therefore to understate the frequency with which fine institutions were almost literally carved out of the wilderness. Images of Victorian palaces of science danced in the heads of museum directors in the hinterland, and they sought to create reasonable facsimiles under adverse circumstances. Some of these museums emphasized local objects, including the artefacts of aboriginal peoples, technological implements, and examples of native flora and fauna. But other museums, especially those associated with universities and colleges, tried to display broad collections, selected to represent the diversity of the animal, vegetable and mineral kingdoms on a worldwide scale.

Like their metropolitan counterparts, colonial museums also set out to educate and morally uplift the middle and lower classes. As one writer described the educational power of natural history specimens: "Let each object represent so much knowledge, to which the very mention of its name will immediately conjure up a crowd of associations, relationships, and intimate acquaintances, and you will then see what a store of real knowledge may be represented in a carefully arranged cabinet." Advocates repeatedly explained that visiting a properly organized natural history museum instilled, in addition to a modicum of scientific information, a sense of order, method, and law. Besides developing an individual's powers of observation and reflection, museums might stimulate healthy exercise. The resultant interest in some branch of natural history could lead the eager student into the "pure air and pleasant scenes" of the countryside, thus offering the "best antidote to habits of dissipation or immorality."[33]

Such frequent and enthusiastic endorsements of the intellectual, social, and moral benefits conferred by natural history museums would seem to indicate that their promoters were not simply mouthing empty rhetoric. As one critic admits, the development of non-art museums has rested on foundations at least potentially more democratic than those supporting art museums.[34] Cathedrals of science were erected as much to fulfil a broad educational aim, however construed by their directors, as to meet the needs of a small coterie of scientific researchers. Perhaps to a greater extent than their colleagues elsewhere, colonial curators brought a missionary zeal to their work, an enthusiasm which implied as well a concern with extending the frontiers of civilization.

COLONIALISM AND SCIENCE

The work of dedicated museum directors and the very act of establishing and sustaining museums in the hinterland may be seen as specific manifestations of a more general historical phenomenon, the growth of colonial science. Most directors were embued with a sense of purpose largely derived from their role as transmitters of scientific culture to an inhospitable environment. Their museums stood as symbols of triumph, not only over intellectual adversity but also over physical, emotional, and moral forces that too often appeared to be in league against them.

Historians have regarded the spread of Western science to other parts of the globe with increasing interest ever since George Basalla wrote his pioneering article on the subject nearly twenty years ago. Basalla proposed a three-stage model, represented by bell-shaped or exponential curves of varying levels of intensity, to describe the transplant of scientific culture from centres where it has flourished to areas where it is virtually unknown. He uses the term "colonial science" only to describe the activity characteristic of his second phase, in which a small group of practitioners depend totally on external scientific traditions and institutions.[35]

According to Basalla, the colonial scientist, whether European or native-born, is educated at least in part abroad. If self-taught, he or she depends on European books, laboratory equipment, and scientific instruments. The strength of these intellectual traditions leads the colonial practitioner to immerse himself in the methods, techniques, and problems of European science. It follows that the colonial scientist seeks honours bestowed by European societies and academies and publishes in established European scientific journals. Basalla's sketch of the colonial scientist describes not simply the psychological profile of an individual, but broader social attitudes engendered by the absence of viable scientific institutions in the hinterland. A concern with natural history typifies the work of the early colonial scientist, although increasingly the range of scientific interests in the colonies expands as the number of practitioners increases during this stage.

Roy MacLeod has recently followed Basalla by supplying another theoretical model — what he calls a framework or "taxonomy" — to describe five major phases of British imperial science between 1780 and 1939. MacLeod has looked at the reverse of Basalla's coin, focusing on imperial connotations rather than colonial implications, and has restricted his purview to one country. Nonetheless, he does pay much attention to the receiving culture and has chosen perhaps the major imperialist / colonizer of all time.[36]

Of MacLeod's five stages, only the second, taking place from the 1830s through the 1870s, is properly called "colonial science." During this period of aggressive metropolitan expansion, a colonial mentality emerged in the hinterland. This spirit emphasized the practical over the theoretical, and accordingly placed a premium on fact-gathering but was characterized above all by a spirit of deference to the mother country. Scientific enterprise nevertheless flowered in the colonies during this phase, as learned societies, universities, museums, and scientific surveys were established and expanded.[37]

Other studies of colonial science, or of science in the service of empire, have turned from Basalla and MacLeod's theoretical models to detailed consideration of particular cases. Michael Worboys examines the five overseas meetings convened by the British Association for the Advancement of Science between 1884 and 1914 and concludes that the science-empire linkage pervaded these meetings. Whether counting the number of papers read on colonial topics, weighing the presence of colonial men of science, or evaluating the scientific advances derived from colonial work, Worboys insists, like his mentor MacLeod, that the relationship between science and imperialism should no longer be ignored.[38]

Ian Inkster scrutinizes the Australian context for virtually the same period as Worboys. He argues that in Australia (contrary to Basalla's model, in which colonial science is replaced by scientific independence) cultural dependency remained high. He concludes that Australian scientists remained peripheral to the cultures of both the mother country and the colony. They were spatially distant from Britain, but mentally isolated from the provincial centres in which they lived and worked.[39]

Daniel Headrick's *Tools of Empire* describes the integral involvement of technology in the extension of imperialist domination. He details how new developments in weaponry, communications, transportation, and medicine worked to give European powers, especially Great Britain, dominion over Africa, India, and China. He, like Basalla and MacLeod, identifies a series of stages in imperial expansion and examines the technologies crucial to each of these steps.[40]

Lucille Brockway, in *Science and Colonial Expansion*, shows how Britain transferred economically useful seeds and plants from sparsely populated "informal" colonies in Latin America to its showcase of empire in Asia, where cultivation became the occupation of a vast pool of underemployed natives. She focuses her study on three cases — cinchona, rubber, and sisal — which she sets in the global context of capital exchange and power politics. According to Brockway, British institutions, particularly the Royal Botanic Gardens at Kew, played a key role in this process, functioning as centres both for research and decision making.[41]

"With the rise of imperialism in the nineteenth century, natural knowledge responded to new sociopolitical and economic arrangements between metropolitan powers and peripheral dependencies," Lewis Pyenson argues in his *Cultural Imperialism and Exact Sciences*. He treats the three principal locations of German expansion in the exact sciences at the beginning of the twentieth century by looking at developments in physics and astronomy in the South Seas, South America, and the Far East. Unlike Headrick and Brockway, Pyenson explores imperialism in the realm of pure sciences, and in particular the establishment of institutions for their propagation.[42]

As the choice of multiple sites of investigation by Headrick, Brockway, and Pyenson would suggest, many studies of scientific colonialism or imperialism are comparative. The historian Raymond Grew has pointed out that colonial topics generally provide fertile ground for comparative history, since new influences and pressures can be identified and their assimilation, distortion, or rejection may be traced.[43] For the historian or sociologist of science in particular, George Basalla maintains that investigations of the diffusion of Western science mark the beginnings of truly comparative studies.

Donald Fleming takes an explicitly comparative approach, trying to understand how far the emergence of vigorous scientific endeavour ran parallel in Australia, Canada, and the United States. According to Fleming, the most powerful impetus to scientific advancement in these three countries was the study of natural history. "It was a fundamental part of the quest for a national identity in societies where the cultural differentiation from Britain was insecure and the sense of the land correspondingly important for self-awareness." Natural history had the added advantage of coinciding with mastering the environment and canvassing its economic potential. Fleming blames the natural history tradition, however, for supplying an inadequate model of science to the colonies. He sees it as bound to "an ethic of practicality and knowledge-for-use," which, in the end, bred an indifference to basic science or pure knowledge.[44]

For Fleming, as for Basalla, MacLeod, and Brockway, colonial practitioners functioned as collectors of facts, while metropolitan scientists acted as theorists or gatekeepers of scientific knowledge. Fleming finds further reason in this to blame the natural history tradition, which permitted the abdication of responsibility to European overlords. This kind of dependence is the very definition of a colonial posture in science for Fleming, since European masters were the only ones allowed to collate the data drawn from colonial experience. Thus, he argues, arises the phenomenon of "absentee lordship" in science. The system does, however, confer certain advantages on the colonist, who is allowed to escape the inevitable storm of controversy that plagues the theorist, although his stake in the scientific enterprise is correspondingly made trivial.[45]

There is, in sum, general agreement on the need to scrutinize the dependency of scientific activity in the hinterland on metropolitan enterprises. The pursuit of natural history in particular has been seen as central in furthering the inequality between centre and periphery. There is also a consensus that historians ought to adopt, if not a strictly comparative approach, at least one that juxtaposes several similar situations. By looking at the development of colonial natural history museums in more than one location and by examining the role of their early directors, it becomes possible to delineate the nature of colonial science at close range.[46]

SOME DESCRIPTIONS OF
COLONIAL MUSEUMS

Historians have largely failed to recognize the extent to which non-European museums of the late nineteenth century tried to assemble significant collections that included prime materials obtained abroad. One justification for museum building was the desire to edify the local populace, especially younger colonists who had never seen the natural and manmade products that were commonplace in Europe. Apart from this rationalization, however, other reasons inspired curators who found themselves working in places and under conditions that they earlier would never have dreamed of. Using European practices and methods as their standards, these men believed that a proper museum had to include objects of universal value as well as materials of local interest alone. The diversity of the natural world was to be shown at least through representative types, if not by a wide variety of individual forms. Their museums' reputations, they felt, depended on the number of specimens amassed, with considerable cachet attached to the acquisition of exotic foreign materials.

If, then, a naturalist's fortune had led him to places like Cape Town or Bombay, the question became (as Melbourne's museum director Frederick McCoy put it) how to *grow* a museum in the hinterland. Growth required money, and funds came to most museums at some stage in their development but rarely at an adequate level or on a regular basis. On the other hand, certain local objects such as rare natural history specimens or archaeological implements had commercial value and might be sold or exchanged for materials from abroad. International exhibitions, whether the huge fairs held in major metropolitan centres or the more modest colonial affairs, called attention to these treasures.

Some colonial museums fared better than others in turning the accidents of nature to good account. The least fortunate were those in Africa, where natural history museums were concentrated in the extreme south. South African and Rhodesian museums survived only in centres with large white populations such as Cape Town, Durban, Pietermaritzburg, and Grahamstown. Although some institutions attempted to attract native inhabitants, more typical, perhaps, was the museum that excluded blacks except on Thursdays, and then required boots or shoes. Even the descendants of English and Dutch settlers failed to attend museums in great numbers because, according to one observer, the magnificent climate vastly outshone the museums' rather unappealing contents. Despite above-average architecture and design, the meagre financial resources of most South African institutions made them impoverished by North American or European standards.[47]

African museums were well endowed, however, compared with their neighbors farther east. The impetus for the creation of a number of India's principal museums — those in Bombay, Calcutta, and Madras — was the donation of the collection of a local philosophical or scientific society. Following the initial bequest, specimens often fell prey to insects and extremes of temperature and humidity. These adverse conditions were exacerbated by poor curatorial care. Hindu workers, reluctant to take life, tended to tolerate pests, while the caste system encouraged a rigid adherence to assigned duties only. In the words of one observer, there was no other place in the world where museums "count[ed] for so little, ... [were] so meagerly supported, or ... [were] so few and far between." Many large towns lacked museums altogether; those that existed were "gingerbread palaces, fantastic and bizarre, or gloomy prisonlike edifices ... [with] galleries more suited to be mausoleums." Some still exhibited freaks and monsters to the curious; others showed obsolete maps and charts, occasionally displayed upside down. As in Africa, widespread illiteracy, extreme poverty, and rural settlement patterns made museums irrelevant to the vast majority of the populace.[48]

Elsewhere, however, the museum movement was more successful. We will examine some of its achievements in North and South America and Australasia. Before proceeding to these specific cases, however, it may be useful to look at museums in general in these three settings.

MUSEUMS IN CANADA, SOUTH AMERICA, AND AUSTRALASIA

The leading museums of post-Confederation Canada were concentrated in a 150-mile radius of Montreal. The largest collections belonged to the museum of the Geological Survey of Canada (later rechristened the National Museum), which was transferred to Ottawa, along with the survey's headquarters, in 1881, after nearly forty years in Montreal. Ottawa's huge reserve of 150,000 paleontological specimens placed it far ahead of any other Canadian museum. Nevertheless, the large number of items displayed in Montreal's Natural History Society Museum, together with McGill University's Peter Redpath Museum, made the city a close second to the national capital. Quebec City, which for a time had alternated with Toronto as capital of the young colony of Canada, placed third because of the excellent collections assembled in the museum of Laval University and in the provincial Museum of Public Instruction.

Although the balance of power would shift away from the province of Quebec with the creation of the Royal Ontario Museum several decades later, Ontario's best museums, those in Kingston and Toronto, housed only a small fraction of the material exhibited in the three main museum centres of Ottawa, Montreal, and Quebec City.[49] The typical Canadian museum of the day — crowded into several rooms, and controlled in Quebec by Catholic educational institutions or by some other kind of organization or university in Ontario — usually contained around 5,000 natural history specimens. Municipal museums, more closely associated with the needs of local citizens than with those of a learned society or school, were almost entirely absent. As one authority who surveyed Canadian museums in the 1930s summed up the case, Canada had long been active in collecting objects for display, but its educational museums were embryonic and its museum endowments negligible.[50]

South American museums, in contrast, tried to function both as research institutions and as instruments of popular enlightenment. Supported by national or provincial governments, important museums could be found in every capital city. Rio de Janeiro, Buenos Aires, Santiago de Chile, and Montevideo erected autonomous natural history museums. Bogota and Caracas combined natural history with art and other subjects and housed all the collections under one roof. Most of these institutions enjoyed comfortable budgets and spacious quarters that accommodated large staffs. They undertook considerable scientific fieldwork and issued a variety of research publications. According to one observer, major museums in South America attracted 100,000 to 150,000 visitors annually, or about 5 to 10 percent of the local population.[51]

Museum resources in Australia and New Zealand compared favorably with those of cities of similar size elsewhere. In New Zealand, as a result of the action of public-spirited and energetic citizens, five towns — Nelson, Christchurch, Wellington, Auckland, and Dunedin — possessed museums by 1877. Australian museums ranged from excellent to mediocre, despite the strong hand of individual state governments in funding. Following settlement patterns, museums tended to be concentrated in the southeastern corner of the mainland. By the 1870s, about a dozen museums, emphasizing geology or zoology, had been created; by 1900 another dozen opened through the efforts of local learned societies.[52]

To generalize from these local variations: the museum movement travelled around the globe with remarkable speed as museums were founded, renovated, or given new quarters everywhere during the last decades of the nineteenth century. The movement's success is especially surprising given the adverse circumstances under which colonial institutions, even in the most favourable situations, had to function. Political and financial problems daily tried the patience of curators like Frederick

McCoy in Melbourne, whose museum fell victim to ministerial whims as internal government reorganizations shuffled it from one department to another. The acute economic depression of the early 1890s caused the dismissal of the entire scientific staff at the Queensland Museum in Brisbane. In Sydney, the acquisitions budget for the Australian Museum was slashed by more than 80 percent.[53]

Acts of God seemed to strike even well-endowed and long-established colonial museums with distressing frequency. Fires destroyed collections at Sydney and at New Westminster, BC, where the entire town went up in flames. Earthquakes wrecked museums in South America and New Zealand. Less extreme circumstances — fluctuations in humidity and temperature, as well as excessive sunlight — caused mounted specimens to shrink, crack, and fade. In tropical areas, damage was also caused by the incursions of moths, mites, birds, and monkeys. By contrast, John William Dawson in Montreal had to contend with a snow blockade that delayed a shipment of materials from New York.[54]

The attitude of the local populace was sometimes just as intractable as the environment. One sympathetic Australian politician complained to McCoy that "it is difficult to indoctrinate people with ideas altogether foreign to those which have already occupied their minds and it is still more difficult to implant a new idea in a mind hitherto fallow."[55] Several curators worried about vandalism and the theft of coins and revolvers because "visitors were too indiscriminately admitted." Indeed, when thieves stole gold from several Australian museums such fears proved to be well founded.[56]

According to those who surveyed colonial museums, themselves museum professionals, the skill and energy of the curatorial staff spelled the difference between success and failure. In South America, a number of Europeans such as Hermann von Ihering in São Paulo and Rudolph Amandus Philippi in Santiago transformed the drudgery of museum building into magnificent testimony to a life's work. In Australia, the sons of prominent British museum curators, such as the Natural History Museum's Henry Woodward and Robert Etheridge, served their scientific apprenticeships as curators at the outposts of the British empire. In many instances, however, the overwhelming problems encountered, and the depressingly low salaries paid, made colonial positions somewhat less than attractive to ambitious naturalists.

To illustrate the early growth of colonial natural history museums, we will look at institutions in five locations: Melbourne, Christchurch, Montreal, Buenos Aires, and La Plata. These particular museums were all directed by unusually active and enthusiastic "museum builders." Early curators stayed at the helm of their museums for decades and during their tenure never failed to bring a single-minded dedication to their work. The fact that these different colonial environments could have produced or attracted such men, who built up remarkably similar institutions, leads one to wonder whether those environments share common characteristics as well.

Scholars have grouped Australia, New Zealand, Canada, and Argentina as hybrid societies, intermediate between development and underdevelopment.[57] With the exception of Argentina, all were colonies or former colonies of Great Britain. Argentina, because of its strong economic ties to Britain, has been seen as part of that country's "informal empire."[58] One author pleads that the historian should "look not at the mere pegging out of claims in African jungles and bush, but at the successful exploitation of the empire, both formal and informal, which was then coming to fruition in ... Latin America, in Canada and elsewhere."[59]

An historian, commenting upon the striking similarities among these societies, notes that "obviously the formal political status of a territory must not be confused with the reality of its position within a wider economic system."[60] Argentina and Canada, for example, were two new favourites on the London money market at the end of the nineteenth century and perhaps exhibit more common features than the more frequently associated "white" British Dominions.[61] The investment of a good deal of British capital during the nineteenth century made Argentina (along with neighboring Uruguay) come to differ greatly from other Latin American countries.[62] On the eve of the First World War, more than one-quarter of total British investment abroad went to Argentina.[63]

It is not surprising that natural history museums enjoyed particular success in environments in which "outposts of transplanted European society" were created. Unlike most other colonial or neocolonial situations, these countries had been settled recently by European immigrants. Native peoples, already decimated or otherwise subjugated, posed no threat to young societies that would come to surpass the living standards of their European progenitors. From around 1870 to 1914, these "Dominion capitalist societies" became the "centre pieces of British imperial strategy." Wool, meat, dairy products, cereals, and lumber were exported from their sparsely settled interiors in return for industrial products, capital, and immigrants. Among the European powers engaged in this process, Great Britain was especially active in financing railroads and other means of transport that helped to get food and raw materials to market.[64] It is not accidental that this period of especially rapid economic growth coincided with the time of museum expansion and that the British imprint on their development was especially strong.[65] As A.F.W. Plumptre has pointed out, a deep reverence for British institutions, whether economic, political, or cultural, as well as a strong sentimental attachment, emerged in these countries.[66]

To focus on a particular set of museums in Canada, South America, and Australasia does not diminish the fact that museums prospered in other colonial locations as well. Both Cape Town's South African Museum and the Indian Museum at Calcutta survive to this day. Even within the "Dominion capitalist societies," museums in other cities, including Sydney, Wellington, and Ottawa, have flourished. One might argue, however, that the patterns of development drawn from the five cases examined in the following pages are typical of the more successful among colonial museums. But precise generalizations will have to wait until historians begin to produce more comprehensive works than commemorative volumes. Rather than merely celebrating the centenary of individual museums, we need to look instead for trends and patterns characteristic of larger groupings of institutions.

In Montreal, greater Buenos Aires, Melbourne, and Christchurch, in any event, enterprising directors found particularly fertile environments for museum-building. Most curators initially emphasized local products and resources, subscribing to the theory that residents were most interested in "the things they can find about home."[67] Attracting as many visitors as possible helped to justify the museums' position as educational institutions. In order to increase popular appeal, directors often displayed coins, ancient relics, and ethnological materials alongside natural history specimens of every description. It was not unusual to show technological apparatus such as agricultural machinery. The particular interests of the director or the contents of a bequest also influenced the composition of collections. As Bather remarked during his survey of colonial institutions, "the first lesson a curator has to learn is to cut his coat according to his cloth." Australian museums, for example, specialized in geological and mineralogical exhibits, while the Canterbury Museum displayed specimens of wool accompanied by practical hints from sheep breeders.[68]

Not for long did colonial curators in these favourable circumstances remain content to direct museums of merely local significance. They sought prime foreign specimens as well, trying to assemble collections to rival those at the great metropolitan museums and to be "to the naturalist what a dictionary is to the scholar."[69] Julius Haast at Christchurch and Frederick McCoy at Melbourne mastered the art of building collections by exchanging or buying specimens abroad. Museums affiliated with local universities, such as the La Plata Museum and the Peter Redpath Museum, aimed to display comprehensive and instructive series of specimens for those who wished to master the rudiments of systematic biology or mineralogy. Several other institutions, including the public museum of Buenos Aires, established solid reputations for scientific research.[70]

The following account begins by considering the people who staffed natural history museums in Christchurch, Melbourne, Montreal, and greater Buenos Aires. It pays special attention to those savants who were, in most cases, imported from abroad to found and develop these institutions. These museum builders — archetypical colonial scientists — accommodated their views about the proper forms and functions of museums to the realities of life in the hinterland. Part of creating a successful enterprise involved finding competent curators, conservators, taxidermists, collectors, and even maintenance workers to perform the many necessary tasks. While some skilled workmen were also brought over from Europe, directors recruited and trained most of their staff from the local labour force.

The second part of the book recounts the histories of these individual museums. Such descriptions show how colonial directors mobilized resources from not-always-eager provincial legislators, national governments, or college trustees. Local architects were hired to realize the museum builders' vision of opulent cathedrals of science. Prevailing opinions about the educational functions of museums, proper methods of displaying specimens, and the uses to which research collections should be put were tailored to fit particular circumstances.

Four of the five museums considered here were supported by provincial governments at some point in their existence. The fifth — the Peter Redpath Museum in Montreal — remained a university museum. All the others, however, forged close ties with local universities. The Redpath Museum, though exclusively a university museum, was the second most important in Canada in its heyday and eclipsed the provincial museum in Quebec. Its status was further increased by the fact that Montreal had at one time served as capital of the province of Canada and never lost much of its political leverage. All five museums, located in important urban centres, functioned in some sense as municipal museums as well.

The third section of the book examines how colonial museums assembled large collections including prime materials obtained from abroad. With either cash or rare specimens to barter, curators entered a complicated system by which natural history materials changed hands. They needed an agent — often a European museum curator — to look after their interests in the open market in specimens, at that time centred in London. This market was dominated by a few leading dealers in natural history objects, who used their businesses to stimulate, and who were in turn sustained by, the Victorian mania for collecting. Colonial museum builders cleverly tapped the acumen of metropolitan curators and dealers in order to put together remarkable inventories. The individual and institutional aspirations that shaped their holdings are also explored.

Colonial museums finally came of age around 1900, in terms of their financial resources, the level of public support, and the size of their holdings. Just at the time when they achieved a measure of independence and international stature, however, the museum movement began to wane all over the world. Some of the reasons why museums in the hinterland began to lose their social, political, and intellectual impact around 1900 are considered in closing.

CHAPTER TWO

Leaders and Followers:
How Museums Were Staffed

It is very difficult to establish museums here in South America. Competent men are totally wanting, and generally the governments, as well as the public, are without the slightest notion of what a Museum ought to be. You cannot have the most remote idea of the difficulties I have met with in a continuous struggle of thirty years to establish the one under my direction; and when I read, as I often do, your observations and counsels on the organization and administration of museums, which you have had the kindness to send me, I am pained at the thought of the difficulties which I shall encounter to attain only a weak imitation of what you would think a museum should be. I have given to the Museum of La Plata my life, my strength, my money, my collections, in fact everything, but I do not feel myself aided. It will be some time before the assistants I have brought together will be able to give efficient aid in the formation of such a scientific institution as I dream of in this extremity of the American continent, and I count upon the kind and amiable cooperation of you my older brother.

Francisco Moreno to George Brown Goode[1]

The presence of a dedicated director was of paramount importance to the success of natural history museums in the hinterland. In this respect, museums — colonial or metropolitan — were like other emerging scientific institutions of the nineteenth century. Surprisingly — even ironically — it seems that as scientists became professionals increasingly specialized and occupying varied positions in new social formations, the role of individual personality became more important. Only those directors who possessed considerable energy and charisma could mobilize the power and financial support necessary for the survival of their museums.[2]

E.P. Alexander uses the phrase "museum masters" to describe the special qualities of those directors who transformed their museums into world-class institutions. He admits that not all great museums were led by a single museum master; the important exceptions include the American Museum of Natural History and Chicago's Field Museum. That museum masters were especially characteristic of the late nineteenth and early twentieth centuries is reflected in the pronouncements of leading museum theorists. The director of the British Museum (Natural History), William Henry Flower, stated simply that "what a museum really depends upon for its success and usefulness is not its building, not its cases, not even its specimens, but its curator. He and his staff are the life and soul of the institution." The Smithsonian Institution's George Brown Goode repeated almost precisely the same sentiment: "A museum without intelligent, progressive, and well-trained curators is as ineffective as a school without teachers, a library without librarians, or a learned society without a working membership of learned men."[3]

Alexander's term "master" carries the connotation of deference, even reverence, that one associates with the *maestro* who leads a symphony orchestra. It is an appropriate and useful term, as it conjures up the vision of deft and delicate orchestration of a multitude of specialized roles. Yet the term "museum builder" perhaps better captures the special place of colonial museum directors who, in every case, produced remarkable institutions from almost nothing.[4] Nearly every conceivable factor — political, economic, or academic — mitigated against the museum builder's success in his undertaking, but remarkable individual perseverance brought eventual triumph over adversity. As well, the *maestro* analogy breaks down because colonial museums often mustered few other permanent staff members. The director's intense commitment to his museum, however, continued unabated for decades.

DIRECTORS

Early directors needed an unwavering sense of purpose in order to wring the resources they needed from parsimonious colonists. Some were especially well suited for this role: Hermann Burmeister (1807-92), Frederick McCoy (1817-99), and Julius Haast (1822-87) all left Europe for positions requiring scientific expertise in the southern hemisphere. Of the three, only Burmeister was hired explicitly to take charge of a natural history museum, in his case at Buenos Aires. Yet the others, like Burmeister, soon made curatorship their principle *raison d'être*. Once they did so, their activism and self-righteousness in this cause often made them seem domineering and uncompromising to their new associates.

Brief Lives

The Irishman Frederick McCoy travelled to Australia in order to assume a new chair of natural sciences at the University of Melbourne. There his ruling passion quickly became the museum that belonged to the young Philosophical Institute of Victoria.[5] He managed to move this museum — just christened the National Museum — to the university grounds and subsequently installed himself as director. To his critics, this was an outrageous act that incensed some of the local inhabitants. To McCoy, however, it was a logical development, as he had established his reputation as a naturalist from classifying the paleontological collections belonging to universities in Dublin, Belfast, and Cambridge.

From a scientific standpoint, Julius Haast's excuse for leaving Germany was less impressive. After having worked for August Krantz of Bonn, a well-known dealer in geological and mineralogical specimens, he was hired to advise an English shipping company on the prospects of German immigration to New Zealand. He went on to explore the geological features of the colony and to receive an appointment as geologist for Canterbury province, a post that he held for seven years. The idea of creating a museum was a natural outgrowth of culling materials from the New Zealand countryside. These objects came to serve Christchurch's Canterbury Museum both as core collections and as the basis for exchange with other institutions.[6]

It is interesting to examine the reasons that compelled these men to travel thousands of miles to the opposite side of the equator. McCoy left a secure post at Queen's College, Belfast, because his large family made the inducement of a fivefold increase in salary especially attractive.[7] From 1856 onwards he earned an additional £300 annually as government paleontologist. (His work as museum director was, however, unpaid.)

Like McCoy, Hermann Burmeister left a university professorship behind him. He left Halle for Argentina and the Buenos Aires Museum, escaping political upheaval in Germany and an unhappy marriage. He possessed the most impressive academic credentials of the group, holding not only a doctorate in philosophy but also a medical degree. Illness compelled him to give up a seat as a representative of the extreme left in the Prussian legislature, and he sought to regain his health by travelling through Brazil, Argentina, and Uruguay during the 1850s. He became so attracted to the South American continent at that time that in the early 1860s he decided to apply (successfully, of course) for the vacant directorship of the Buenos Aires Museum.

Unlike his countryman, Julius Haast had pursued only desultory studies in geology and mineralogy at the university level. A voyage to New Zealand offered an exciting alternative to Haast's "somewhat undistinguished life gripped by wanderlust," as well as a chance to efface the untimely death of his first wife.[8] Like Burmeister, Haast found a new mate in his adoptive homeland.

The strong, if idiosyncratic, personalities of these émigrés made them a source of great interest to more staid local inhabitants. Despite widespread disapproval of his unorthodox behaviour, the exploits of the debonair and dashing McCoy captivated Victoria's press. McCoy, who diligently exercised with heavy dumbbells each morning, was famous for illustrating his lectures with mineral specimens which, when he tossed them to a student, fell crashing to the floor. Contemporaries viewed the autocratic dispositions of German-born Burmeister and Haast with less affection. Burmeister's irrascibility quickly became a legend in Argentina. One observer described this "courteous but independent autocrat" as "spare and tall, eagle-eyed, [and] fibrous, his whole frame bristling with intellectual energy." In New Zealand, Haast's willingness to sing in public and play the violin appeared to temper his dogmatism. An historian describes him as "a huge, jovial explorer whose enthusiasms took him happily among the icy peaks of the Southern Alps ... his dominating, extrovert warm nature must have stirred the socially correct Christchurch society of Victorian days."[9]

Francisco Moreno (1852-1919) and John William Dawson (1820-99) stayed in their home countries, but both spent several years in Europe, where they were inspired by major natural history museums. Moreno and Dawson assembled extensive paleontological collections of their own, and these served as the core of the museums that they would eventually direct. Dawson, coming to Lower Canada from Nova Scotia in 1855 to be principal of McGill College, found perhaps his most congenial pursuit in Montreal to be the establishment of the Peter Redpath Museum. For Moreno, the creation of a new national capital at La Plata in 1882 and the subsequent foundation of the La Plata Museum gave him the dreamed-of chance to transform his modest anthropological cabinet into a scientific showcase for the whole of Argentina.

McCoy, Burmeister, Haast, Dawson, and Moreno, despite their different backgrounds and the diverse circumstances in which they lived, shared many common characteristics. As Donald Fleming remarks in his discussion of scientific parallels in nineteenth-century Canada, Australia, and the United States, "cognate figures prosecuting the same researches in the same spirit can readily be identified in the three communities."[10] In the case of the men treated here, all became directors at the museum's foundation or shortly thereafter, and they stayed for decades. Usually only death could stop their myriad activities that reached feverish pitch in supervising a natural history museum. One biographer described McCoy as "fiery, impulsive, resilient, unsuited to collective enterprises,"[11] and the same might be said of the others.

Intellectual Interests

By George Basalla's criteria, early museum directors functioned as almost archetypal "colonial scientists." Their lives revolved around creating those "institutions and traditions which will eventually provide the basis for an independent scientific culture."[12] They directed their energies toward establishing and promoting scientific journals and other publications, learned societies, and educational institutions in the hinterland. In addition, all possessed an encyclopedic range of scientific interests and the willingness to pursue them with remarkable enthusiasm.

They were good generalists at a time when specialists in botany, zoology, and geology were beginning to replace the all-around naturalists of earlier days. Dawson, for example, published an average of ten papers a year on diverse scientific topics and probably a similar number on educational, social, and religious matters. Besides his work in geology and paleontology, he undertook studies in invertebrate zoology and agriculture. Burmeister also wrote voluminously on many branches of science, including entomology, zoology, paleontology, geology, geography, meteorology, and physics. Confronted by a shortage of trained technical artists in Argentina, he even illustrated some of his own works, including the Buenos Aires Museum's *Anales*. Like Dawson, he also tried his hand at the popularization of science. Entomology received the greatest share of his attention; he wrote seventy-five papers in the field, as well as a five-volume *Handbuch der Entomologie* (1832-47), a work which became a definitive source for entomologists. In Australia, Haast published on topics in botany, anthropology, geology, and paleontology, and also helped to found and administer a range of cultural institutions in his adoptive city. Dawson was creating the same kinds of organizations at about the same time, thousands of miles away in Montreal.[13]

These broad scientific interests notwithstanding, those who directed natural history museums in the hinterland made their mark as geologists and paleontologists. As the botanist and director of Kew Gardens, Sir Joseph Hooker, wrote to Haast in the late 1860s, "Geology, as a science, has had lately the plums of the small cake that is divided amongst the scientific men — and the fairly well paid colonial appointments given to geologists have been quite exceptional."[14] In addition to their museum responsibilities, each director taught geology and paleontology at the local university.

Colonial curators made important contributions to the growing literature in these specialities. Dawson's fieldwork made him one of the leading authorities on the geology of Eastern Canada and expanded the number of known post-Pliocene fossil types from around 30 to more than 200. His efforts in the realm of paleozoology extended from the lowest forms of life to prehistoric man and included Cambrian sponges, postglacial Arctic fauna, the earliest land snails, fossil amphibia, and fossil reptiles. His work was especially acclaimed (and less controversial) in the area of paleobotany, in which he published several articles every year as well as a textbook, *The Geological History of Plants*. Trilobites were Hermann Burmeister's paleontological specialty, while Moreno became an expert on the Tertiary fauna of Patagonia. Haast earned praise for his pioneering work on the stratigraphy, volcanic activity, and glacial phenomena of New Zealand. McCoy established himself as an authority on British Carboniferous and Silurian fossils, publishing twenty-eight articles on these topics in the prestigious *Annals and Magazine of Natural History* over less than a decade. In that journal he had even discussed the fossil record of Australia before ever setting foot on the continent.[15]

Not surprisingly, Dawson, McCoy, and Haast each played an important role in the recently created geological surveys of their respective country, state, and province. Dawson and McCoy's geological knowledge of their colonies led them into mining speculation and, in McCoy's case, to the loss of his fortune. McCoy also misled Australian miners about the likelihood of striking gold. On a more positive note, Haast, renowned for his systematic study of New Zealand geology, discovered a lucrative coal seam near the town of Nelson, north of Christchurch.[16] As contemporaries and historians alike have pointed out, financial support for colonial science was usually contingent upon practical success in its application. Museum builders were not slow to appreciate the connection between the exploitation of natural resources and public appreciation for museums where minerals and other natural history objects would be displayed.

Perhaps because of their detailed knowledge of the paleontological and geological record, Dawson, Burmeister, and McCoy became outspoken critics of Darwinian evolution. All were part of the older generation of naturalists which Darwin had not expected to convince.[17] Darwin described Dawson to his confidant Joseph Dalton Hooker as "the staunchest of creationists."[18] He had heard, correctly as it turned out, that Dawson would review the *Origin of Species*, and from "so biased a judge … no spirit of fairness can be expected."[19] Hooker concurred that Dawson "seems to hate Darwinism."[20] Eventually Dawson wrote numerous anti-Darwinian polemical tracts and acquired the reputation as the only scientist in North America who had not "bowed the knee" to evolution.[21]

Hermann Burmeister was just as inflexible. He upheld the doctrine of catastrophist geology, especially a variety called vulcanism, which emphasized the role of volcanoes in shaping the earth. He dismissed

Darwinian evolution as a mere hypothesis in edition after edition of his *History of Creation*, first published in 1843.[22] McCoy, as a Roman Catholic turned devout Anglican, like the staunchly Presbyterian Dawson, sought to reconcile an understanding of the natural world with Scripture.[23] In 1870, he lectured to a Melbourne audience for three hours on the "Order and Plan of Creation," a talk which challenged the veracity of the decade-old and by then widely accepted *Origin of Species*.[24] McCoy argued that paleontology supported not only the doctrine of special creation in general but a special creation of Australian mammals in particular. McCoy's ardent anti-evolutionism found favour with the conservative, church-going public in Melbourne, while leaving a handful of more progressive Australian scientists less impressed.[25]

A concern with the question of the antiquity of man may have been responsible for shifting the interests of directors towards ethnology, anthropology, and archaeology, all of which became notable areas of museum expansion in later years.[26] Indeed, generally speaking, museum holdings often complemented the scholarly interests of their builders. This came about partly because research agendas usually were dictated by available resources. Haast, for example, became a leading authority on the extinct moa bird and the aboriginal tribes that he believed had hunted it. This interest was fueled by the periodic excavation of bones and implements nearby; these served as the basis of the Canterbury Museum's collections and the source for exchanges with other institutions.

It was not unusual, however, for directors to shape museum inventories in order to support their favorite scientific concerns. McCoy built up the National Museum's collection of Silurian fossils so that he might finish studies on that formation that he had begun before his arrival in Australia. His reputation as a paleontologist had rested upon museum studies, not fieldwork, ever since his employment as Adam Sedgwick's assistant in the Woodwardian geological museum at Cambridge University.[27] In Argentina, the eminent geologist and paleontologist Florentino Ameghino accused Burmeister of improving the Buenos Aires Museum's paleontological collections for his own exclusive use. Burmeister, in his defense, claimed that upon accepting the directorship of the Argentine museum, he had resolved to devote himself entirely to the study of the natural history of that country.[28]

Controversy and Contentions

Acrimonious controversy was another characteristic common to curators working in the hinterland. Dawson became an ardent champion of the organic nature of a puzzling Precambrian fossil fragment called *Eozoön canadense*, popularized as the "dawn animal" of Canada. Dawson's dogmatism nonetheless failed to persuade the scientific community, which eventually concluded that the specimen was only a rock. Julius Haast took on not only his fellow curator in New Zealand, James Hector, but also the French doyen of anthropology, Jean-Louis-Armand de Quatrefages, in a dispute about the age of the so-called "moa hunters," a dispute which Haast ultimately lost. McCoy quibbled for thirty years with the Reverend William Branwhite Clarke over the dating of New South Wales coal deposits and refused to concede defeat despite mounting evidence against him.[29] There was no one with whom colonial curators hesitated to join battle, whether metropolitan luminary or provincial nobody.[30]

In Argentina, institutional rivalry only served to enflame the considerable personal animosity and intellectual disagreement that had already developed between the strong-willed Francisco Moreno and the cantankerous Hermann Burmeister. The most vicious dispute erupted between the two museum directors and Florentino Ameghino, who attacked both men as representatives of "official" science. Burmeister took up the gauntlet in his *Anales del Museo Público* (and in *Sur quelques genres de mammifères fossiles*), where he challenged in particular Ameghino's transformist, materialist views. Ameghino, for his part, charged that Burmeister wrote out of jealousy of Ameghino's greater accomplishments in the area of paleontological and anthropological research that both naturalists shared. During Burmeister's thirty-year directorship of the Buenos Aires Museum, argued Ameghino, not only had he shaped and exploited the collections for his own research, but he also had failed to train a single disciple. The Argentine-born Ameghino castigated Burmeister for his Germanness and complained to his friends of the spirit of "extranjerismo" (fondness for things foreign) invading the country. Argentina, wrote Ameghino's confidant Victor Mercante, is "a fickle child who scorns her sons in order to caress foreigners."[31]

Ameghino reserved his most vituperative comments for his fellow Argentinian, Francisco Moreno, to whom he served as assistant and secretary at the La Plata Museum for a year and a half. Ameghino and Moreno had earlier disagreed over interpreting the fossil record, but their personal relationship deteriorated further at the museum. For reasons that are still not clear, Ameghino was summarily dismissed from his post, lost his university position in the local faculty of sciences, and was banned from entry to the museum. As a result of these reserves, Ameghino came to refer to Moreno as the most egotistical man who ever lived, and as someone who, like Burmeister, saw the museum as his own personal property.[32]

The viciousness of the quarrels among museum men in Argentina may seem remarkable, but other colonial curators also felt the long-term effects of petty political struggles, notable for their ongoing displays of ill will and bitterness. The careers of McCoy and Dawson, both prod-ucts of the British scientific system, exhibit especially strong parallels in this regard. Both men, despite powerful patrons, were denied posi-tions that they sought vigorously in Britain during the 1840s and 1850s. McCoy, for example, had joined the large number of men vying for the curatorship of the Geological Society vacated by William Lonsdale in 1842.[33] He lost out to Edward Forbes in the end, just as Dawson would a decade later when he applied for the chair in natural history at Edin-burgh. During the early 1850s, McCoy tried unsuccessfully to obtain a post at the British Museum. This he lost despite the considerable sup-port of Adam Sedgwick, to whom he had earlier been assistant at the Cambridge geological museum.[34]

Like Sedgwick, Dawson's patron Charles Lyell was an enemy of the powerful Roderick Impey Murchison, director general of the Geological Survey of Great Britain. Both Sedgwick and Lyell felt that Murchison's influence had weighed unfairly against their protégés.[35] McCoy con-tended that Murchison had never forgiven him for his unwavering sup-port of Sedgwick during the notorious dispute over the Cambrian–Silu-rian boundary. As a result, asserted McCoy, Murchison "did him much mischief at times."[36] McCoy would have liked to succeed Edward Forbes as paleontologist to the geological survey, but he later wrote of "the whole might of the staff," led by Murchison, being used against him.[37]

Like McCoy, Dawson felt that he was persecuted by institutionalized "official" British science on more than one occasion. The University of Edinburgh declined his services for a second time when he sought the principalship there in 1866. In a breach of tradition without precedent, the Royal Society of London refused to publish his Bakerian lecture of 1870 on Devonian plants in its *Philosophical Transactions*. Dawson's indig-nant response was to "throw no more of my pearls before the swine in that quarter."[38]

The background to this particular incident reveals the narrow path that colonial scientists were expected to follow and demonstrates the sanctions that could be applied against them, if they strayed. In May 1870, the Royal Society asked the newly knighted Sir Joseph Hooker to referee Dawson's paper. The choice was unfortunate from Dawson's perspective, since the two scientists had clashed eight years earlier when (as Hooker put it) Dawson had "poohpoohed his Greenland paper."[39] Hooker, pronouncing Dawson's paper "so full of perfect trash," explained in more detail to Darwin that, although Dawson's discovery of Carboniferous fossil plants in the Devonian stratum was excellent, he had unfortunately failed to content himself "with the proper summation of that." Dawson's paper was a disaster, argued Hooker, and he was forced to recommend that it not be published. His review was remarkably harsh, coming from a time when scientists were expected to adhere to a strict gentlemanly code of conduct. Of Dawson's paper, Hooker wrote Darwin: "The systematic part is very meagre indeed, the vegetable anatomy miserable and often utterly wrong; the affinities more often mere guess work than not; and as to the theories and speculations, they would make your hair stand on end."[40]

One senses from the Darwin–Hooker correspondence that there was no love lost between Dawson and the two British naturalists. One of the roots of the problem was undoubtedly Dawson's outspoken anti-evolutionism, which annoyed his British colleagues.[41] In addition, Hooker and Darwin seem to have disliked Dawson, especially his egotistical personality.[42] Still, the fervour with which Hooker denounced Dawson's work is almost jarring. Hooker seemed especially incensed that Dawson should theorize instead of remaining content with the factual. Maybe he thought that Dawson was violating the norms of Baconian induction, or perhaps he felt that Dawson, coming "all the way from Canada," was embarking upon territory where he should not trespass.[43] He complained again in the same letter to Darwin that Dawson's work contained "page after page of the wildest speculations upon *Archaea* and *synthetic* types, on *origination of species*, etc."[44]

It is equally revealing that Hooker recognized the consequences of his action for Dawson's future scientific career; he was dealing it a murderous stroke. He reiterated several times that his criticism would mean a "knock down blow to the poor man," "whose fall will be proportionally heavy and headlong." Hooker claimed that he would "rather have burnt my fingers than performed so hateful a duty," which was made worse by the fact that Dawson's wife was pretty and his son deformed. As a result, exclaimed Hooker, "the curse of Cain will cleave to me."[45]

Clearly, some scientists are more powerful and influential than others. Sedgwick and Lyell seemed to have been no match for the combined forces of Murchison, Hooker, and Darwin. One suspects, too, that negative appraisals like those meted out by Hooker to Dawson and Henri Milne-Edwards to McCoy could scarcely be annulled by even the most positive recommendations. Dawson and McCoy continued to correspond with their patrons for years, coming to them for solace, advice, and support until both mentors were incapacitated by old age and infirmity. McCoy complained only to Sedgwick, for example, of being overworked and underpaid, of his intense nostalgia for England, and of conditions in Australia that he found depressing.[46] Their protégés' perseverance against seemingly insurmountable physical and psychological odds tremendously impressed the two older men. According to Sedgwick, McCoy had the "greatest working power of all the men of science I ever met with."[47]

Because recognition and recompense were strenuously sought but rarely achieved, colonial museum directors treasured their honours and awards, especially those bestowed by European courts and academies. The directors who lacked university degrees were perhaps particularly desirous to add extra initials and titles to their names. Although one of his correspondents argued "what is knighthood or decoration in comparison with the bona fide applause of the real leaders of science," the German-born Haast was elated to receive an Austrian knighthood. He even insisted that schoolmates address his children with the newly acquired "von."[48] The knighthood came to him in 1874 because he had dedicated and donated special collections of remains of the extinct moa bird to the Austrian royal family. Afterwards he decided to ship other prime moa specimens to Alphonse Milne-Edwards in Paris at the latter's hint of a membership in the French Académie des sciences.[49] In 1891 Frederick McCoy, who also lacked a university degree, became the first Australian professor to be knighted.[50] In Montreal, Dawson found the receipt of his knighthood in 1884, two years after opening the Redpath Museum and on the eve of welcoming the British Association for the Advancement of Science to their first overseas meeting, to be one of the happiest moments of his life.

The foibles, quirks, and disappointments of these museum builders take on special significance because the imprint of their personalities on colonial museum development was so strong. In the long run, however, the domination of the directors was a liability. Museum fortunes were tied to the vigour of their leadership, and as physical and mental infirmity set in (as it did for almost all of these men around 1890), the museums likewise began to decline. With the exception of Dawson, perhaps, museum builders worked in isolation and failed to train a corps of properly educated disciples to replace them.[51] The chronic shortage of funds, which resulted in a staff insufficient both in numbers and scientific expertise, further accentuated the administrative and intellectual domination of the director. (Nor were directors themselves pleased to find that their own research activities were curtailed by the demands of museum administration.)[52] For the institution, recovery was difficult once firm guidance from above faltered after decades of authoritarian direction.

SUPPORT STAFF

No matter how charismatic, energetic, or powerful he was, no museum director could function without staff to support his efforts. In his 1895

Table 1
Number of Paid Museum Staff and Salary Expenses

Museum	1870	1875	1880	1885	1890
Canterbury					
Staff	—	—	—	—	2[2]
Salaries (£)	650	1,110[1]	1,011	1,074	—
Victoria					
Staff	6	6	—	—	11
Salaries (£)	1,205	1,365	1,365	1,405	1,836[3]
Redpath					
Staff	—	—	2	2	2
Salaries ($Cdn)	—	—	900	940	940
Buenos Aires					
Staff	4	5	4	5	7
Salaries (pesos)[4]	90,000	165,600	116,400	6,084	—
La Plata					
Staff	—	—	—	9	—
Salaries (pesos)[4]	—	—	—	9,324	—

[1] In 1877
[2] In 1900
[3] In 1893
[4] Beginning in 1885, Argentinian museums received allocations in silver pesos rather than paper (£1 = approx. 120 paper pesos = approx. 5 silver pesos)

Sources: BAM, File M; LPM, law of the Province of Buenos Aires, no. 1.816, 17 June 1886; Universidad Nacional de La Plata, *Obra del centenario del Museo de La Plata* (La Plata: Facultad de Ciencias Naturales y Museo 1977), vol. 1, *Reseña Historica*, 9; H.F. von Haast, *Life and Times of Sir Julius von Haast* (Wellington, NZ: Avery Press 1948), 884, 887; TL, folder 23, notebook re Canterbury Museum; NMV, letterbooks 2, 3; annual *Report ... of the Public Library, Museums, and Natural Gallery of Victoria*; F.A. Bather, "Some Colonial Museums," Museums Association, *Report of Proceedings ... 1894 ... in Dublin* (London: Museums Association 1895); *Minerva: Jahrbuch der gelehrten Welt* (Strasbourg: Karl J. Trübner 1891 –).

essay on museum administration, George Brown Goode stressed the importance of "competent" curators, suggesting that each should be an authority on some specialized field of research.[53] For colonial museums, however, this kind of professional expertise in a range of posts was an almost unthinkable luxury. Since staffing, like all expenditure on museums, required persuading tightfisted legislators or trustees to part with their money, directors were lucky to be able to hire a few self-taught workers who were willing to perform a variety of tasks.

The governments or universities that supported museums recognized, however, that the initial agreement to fund permanent employees tied up resources for years to come. This development made a financial com-

Table 2
Museum Expenditures

Museum	1860	1865	1870	1875	1880	1885	1890
Canterbury							
(£)	—	—	1,000	1,500	1,800	1,400	—
Victoria							
(£)	2,000	3,900	2,500	—	—	—	1,800
Redpath							
($Cdn)	—	—	—	—	1,130	1,925	1,215
(£)	—	—	—	—	226	385	243
Buenos Aires							
pesos[1]	—	50,000	100,000	190,000	134,000	8,499	—
(£)	—	431	862	1,551	1,094	1,700	—
La Plata							
(pesos)[1]	—	—	—	—	—	15,944	—
(£)	—	—	—	—	—	3,189	—

[1] Beginning in 1885, Argentine museums received allocations in silver pesos rather than paper (£1 = approx. 120 paper pesos = approx. 5 silver pesos)

Sources: TL, notebook concerning the Canterbury Museum, MS papers 37, folder 23; R.T.M. Pescott, *Collections of a Century: the History of the First Hundred Years of the National Museum of Victoria* (Melbourne: National Museum of Victoria, 1954), 44; NMV, letterbook 3, 75, "Return of the National Museum for 1865"; ibid, 365, "Return ... for 1869." *Report ... of the Public Library, Museums, and National Gallery of Victoria for 1890*, 8–9; BAM, file M for 1865; 5 May 1870, Burmeister to Ministerio de Gobernio; BAM, "Cuenta del Museo Público para el año 1875," 1876, fol. 467; BAM, "Cuento de gastos para el Museo Público durante el año 1880," 1881, fol. 543; BAM, "Cuenta para el año 1884 del Museo Público," fol. 787; BAM, Burmeister to Filemon Posse, 1 March 1890; JWD, acc. 1459, 1, Redpath Museum minute book, 1892–1917, 33, 47–66, 119–30; LPM, folder of documents on the museum, law of the Province of Buenos Aires, no. 1.816, 17 June 1886.

mitment to personnel a fundamentally different kind of investment from construction which, though expensive, ended with the building's completion, renovation, or addition. Not only were staff salaries an ongoing expense, but comparing Table 1 with Table 2 shows that, for any given year, the largest single portion of a museum's budget went to salaries. In the case of the Buenos Aires Museum with an especially large staff (as for the Peter Redpath Museum with a particularly small one) this proportion amounted to 90 percent. Even the National Museum of Victoria, which according to critics had neglected to hire the necessary complement of curatorial staff, spent around 50 percent of its budget on this item alone.[54]

Probably because of the considerable financial outlay required, in the long or short term, colonial museums lagged most clearly behind major metropolitan institutions in the realm of personnel. New York's American Museum of Natural History, for example, included fourteen scientists (among a total of seventy-one employees) in 1877, around the same time that the British Museum (Natural History) had a scientific staff of thirteen assistants and seventeen attendants. In contrast, Argentine museums mustered staffs of eight or nine members by the late 1880s, and this was an exceptionally large number for a colonial institution. Other museums, such as the Redpath Museum and the Canterbury Museum, never hired more than a handful of permanent employees. As a result, the ability to exploit local talent on a casual basis became essential for most museums in the hinterland.

Since all colonial museums suffered from a shortage of skilled workers during their early years, their staffs bore certain strong resemblances to each other. Directors were not afraid to assume a variety of duties, from looking after several departments to (on occasion) sweeping the floors.[55] Because of their limited numbers, subordinate staff also became adept at a range of functions. Even those young men lacking special training could rise very quickly in museum hierarchies, carving out a niche in the organization and a new career at the same time.

Given their limited funds and the absence of local institutions for training curators and naturalists, colonial museums fared surprisingly well in recruiting competent and loyal staff members. Two developments were responsible. First, metropolitan markets could absorb only some of the young men schooled by natural history suppliers and taxidermy firms such as Ward and Howell or the Verreaux brothers in Paris.[56] It was not unusual, therefore, for new graduates to seek their fortunes in the hinterland. As an added inducement, they might collect exotic specimens on the side, and these would fetch handsome prices when shipped back home. A second reason for the surprisingly high level of proficiency among museum staff was a healthy smattering of untrained talent in the immediate community. Those hired to fill even menial museum positions often advanced through the ranks, where eventually they learned new skills. This evolution occurred out of necessity, but also because local recruits were enterprising enough to turn on-the-job training to good account.

Those curators with the most money at their disposal tended first to look abroad for scientific staff. Hermann Burmeister imported the Buenos Aires Museum's first preparators, Antonio Pozzi and his son Santiago, from Italy.[57] Santiago eventually went on to the La Plata Museum, where he worked for fourteen years and earned a reputation as being the best museum technician in the country.[58] Museum inspectors Balthazar Triebling and Carlos Berg, next in rank to Burmeister and acting as his assistants, were recruited from Austria and Russia. One of the few Spaniards involved in the natural history trade in Argentina or elsewhere was the interim conservator and collector Enrique de Carles from Barcelona. In Australia, where taxidermy was in its infancy, McCoy hired the son of a famous London natural history dealer, John Leadbeater, Jr.[59]

One of the many taxidermists sent out from Henry Ward's "natural science establishment" in Rochester to join the staff of museums and colleges was Jules Bailly, a specialist in mounting skeletons, whom Ward had imported from the Verreaux firm. He was responsible for training a whole generation of American conservators. Perhaps it was his French background that persuaded Bailly to join Dawson in Montreal.[60] Ward sent another trainee to New Zealand, C.F. Adams, who ended up at the natural history museum in Auckland.[61] Yet another taxidermist travelling to New Zealand was Andreas Reischek from Vienna. At Christchurch he shared a common language with museum director Haast, but Reischek's unorthodox behaviour soured the relationship between the two men.[62]

Failing the resources or connections to recruit employees abroad, directors next turned to the community. Since no one there was actually qualified to fill a museum position, posts were accessible to anyone. Jobs requiring manual labour were generally filled by men from the lower social classes. In Montreal, for example, Paul Kuetzing, employed by a piano factory, spent his spare time preparing specimens for the Redpath Museum. The first taxidermist employed at the National Museum of Victoria, George Fulker, had originally trained as a shoemaker.[63]

For these men, advancement through the museum ranks was both possible and probable. In Christchurch, William Sparkes, Jr., started out as assistant to Reischek and later replaced him as taxidermist and general factotum of the museum.[64] The Redpath Museum's janitor, Edward Ardley, became so adept at caring for the collections that he gradually took over the job of assistant curator. At the Buenos Aires Museum, after four years as porter (during which time he also collected for the museum on a casual basis), the Frenchman José Monquillot became preparator in 1875.[65]

In many instances, fathers trained their sons with a view to their succession. James Kershaw was the son of the National Museum of Victoria's taxidermist William Kershaw, and became his assistant in 1883.[66] In Montreal, both Edward Ardley's son and his father were hired from time to time to stoke the furnace, shovel snow, and dust the collections at the Redpath Museum. Though colonial museums had trouble in obtaining qualified staff as in other respects, gradually they built up a reservoir of good, self-taught workers.

TWO CASES:
THE PETER REDPATH MUSEUM
AND THE BUENOS AIRES MUSEUM

We can examine the range in possible staffing arrangements adopted by colonial museums by comparing two institutions at opposite ends of the spectrum in terms of resources and number of staff. Montreal's Redpath Museum, a university museum operating with severely limited finances throughout its history, depended on the goodwill of a number of supporters in the local community. Its relatively open organization absorbed volunteers and low-paid but enthusiastic workers into its ranks. By way of contrast, the Buenos Aires Museum, moderately well funded (despite the complaints of its director), displayed a rigidly hierarchical organization with all power and decision making residing at the top.

The permanent staff of the Redpath Museum during its first several decades consisted of two men. One was the assistant curator, Thomas Curry, who earned around $500 a year from the special fund endowed for this purpose by Louisa Molson, wife of a Montreal brewing magnate. Curry took charge of mounting, labelling, arranging, cataloguing, and (on occasion) collecting specimens. The museum caretaker, Edward Ardley, worked at first for just $30 a month plus free lodging in a heated flat in the museum basement.

Over the years that Ardley tended the museum, his tasks became increasingly skilled and specialized. In 1886, the museum committee bought him a set of carpenter's tools to help him build display stands and shelves. Three years later, Ardley regularly cleaned and mounted specimens, owing to the increasing size of the collections and to Curry's failing health. He also learned to operate a lathe in order to slice sections of rocks and fossils. When Curry died in the spring of 1894, Ardley took charge of the museum specimens and earned the new title of "caretaker and museum assistant" along with a modest pay increase.[67] Not until 1906, however, was he permitted to relinquish the post of janitor and to live outside the museum building. Five years later, he had picked up further skills as a collector of fossils and rocks and as a preparator of ethnological materials.

In order for the museum to function, given the limited size of its staff, Dawson depended upon this adaptability among his permanent employees. In addition, he fully exploited the institution's association with McGill University. Anyone hired as a lecturer or professor of natural history sciences at the university was expected to act as a volunteer curator for the materials in his department of the museum. In 1883 the new professor of botany, David Penhallow, joined Dawson and a professor of chemistry and mineralogy, Bernard J. Harrington, at the

Redpath Museum. Penhallow laboured indefatigably to build up the museum's herbarium. A decade later, Frank Dawson Adams succeeded Dawson as Logan Professor of Geology, and he, too, took an active role in shaping the museum's geological department. Adams generously presented hundreds of his own specimens, as well as a large number of geological photographs.

Subsequent teaching positions in natural history at McGill were created in part because of the pressure exerted by the museum on university priorities. The zoology lectureship was elevated to a professorship in 1897 after Dawson (by then retired as McGill's principal) urged the change for the benefit of the museum's holdings in this department. The position fell to E.W. MacBride instead of W.R. Deeks, who had worked his way through the ranks of zoology preparator, demonstrator, lecturer, and instructor, only to resign because of the demands of his medical practice.[68] Around this time, Jules Bailly, a temporary employee of the museum for the previous ten years, gained a permanent post as osteologist under the joint direction of the Faculty of Medicine and the Redpath Museum.[69]

Other hands were hired on a casual basis to carry out specific assignments. Several McGill graduates volunteered to arrange, label, and catalogue collections of insects and fossils. Ward and Howell set up a gorilla skeleton acquired from Liverpool, although Dawson rejected, on grounds of economy, an accompanying black walnut pedestal and brass accessories. Generally, however, the firm's former employee, Bailly, acted as resident taxidermist on a per specimen basis. To him fell the task of mounting the skeleton of a bison shot by J.H.R. Molson (Louisa's husband) and Dawson somewhere between Calgary and Medicine Hat.[70] Another Montrealer, George Roberts, constructed display cases for the growing collections. When the museum lacked $600 to purchase cases for some of the botanical specimens, Roberts's offer to defer payment was eagerly accepted. Unfortunately for the poor carpenter, a year elapsed before he received even half the amount owed to him.[71]

The practice of exploiting local talent on an *ad hoc* basis — whether the guidance of McGill professors or the ingenuity of Edward Ardley — undermined Dawson's plea for a larger and better-trained permanent staff. Although Dawson commended Ardley and thanked his colleagues for their help and skill in collecting, preparing, mounting, labelling, renovating, and arranging specimens, he still wanted a "paid scientific curator" to classify specimens, exchange materials with other institutions, and supervise students.[72] But no such appointment was made after Thomas Curry died, at which time the fund covering his stipend lapsed. Clearly the Redpath Museum could function adequately without a full-time curator, the McGill Board of Governors must have reasoned, given Dawson's astute allocation of existing resources.

The meagre size and funding of the staff of the Redpath Museum may be contrasted to the Buenos Aires Museum, which employed a considerable variety of personnel over the years. In his early accounts in the *Anales del Museo Público* in 1864, Burmeister complained that he had no help at the museum except for the porter, who cleaned the rooms and on occasion helped arrange the collections.[73] By 1871, however, an inspector, conservator, and hunter were added to the permanent staff. The inspector acted as assistant to Burmeister until the abolition of the post in 1876. The position was reinstated five years later, at which time the incumbent was ordered to supervise the library rather than the collections.[74] This new directive matched Burmeister's emphasis on the importance of the library.

As at the Redpath Museum, lesser positions at the Buenos Aires Museum came to require expertise in a range of areas. The conservator was called upon to fill half a dozen jobs, serving as sculptor, maker of casts and models, illustrator, and photographer, in addition to preparing specimens.[75] The hunter not only caught birds but also acted as assistant to the conservator by mounting skeletons, designing pedestals, and shaping supports for animals.

Despite the assistance of a staff of up to seven, Burmeister resisted the notion of delegating authority to his subordinates. Even in domains outside his own special research interests, such as ornithology, Burmeister took charge of arranging the collections throughout his directorship. In 1874 he claimed that he was so busy restoring fossils for the museum that he had time neither for his own research nor to continue overseeing publication of the museum's official journal, the *Anales*.[76] This contraction in the range of museum activities occurred, not surprisingly, just at the time when the government began to cut its allocations.

Burmeister's salary, originally set at 1,000 pesos a month, increased eight times in his first decade at the museum. The inspector, the next most highly paid employee, earned only about one-third as much as the director. Next came the conservator and hunter, each paid about one-eighth Burmeister's salary. Among the casual employees were carpenters, bookbinders, and blacksmiths (who forged display stands for specimens). This pay range corresponded to the rigidly hierarchical organization commanded by Burmeister.

Burmeister laboured long over decisions about the pay, hiring, or firing of his staff. He sternly decreed, for example, that all employees who did not report to work during the cholera epidemic of 1867 would lose their jobs.[77] Shortly after the Pozzis asked for a raise in 1868, they were fired.[78] Burmeister sought the dismissal of conservator Alberto Neuto after a mere six months on the job, because his work seemed inartistic and crude to the demanding director.[79]

Nevertheless, over time, Burmeister began to mellow. He became especially sympathetic to the financial plight of his employees. During most of his directorship, he allowed the collector, Dr. Luis Moser, to supplement his salary by serving as night watchman for the museum. When the government abolished the post of collector in 1876, Burmeister asked instead that the inspectorship be sacrificed, as the holder of that position had already accepted a university professorship. This alternative, Burmeister felt, would be less hard on the morale of his staff.[80] When conservator José Monquillot threatened to resign in 1883, Burmeister augmented his salary out of a special appropriation.[81]

During times of budgetary contraction, Burmeister became especially sensitive to inequities and reductions in the pay of his staff. He continually objected to the unreasonable practice of paying equal salaries to the conservator and the hunter, when the latter acted as assistant to the former.[82] Besides increasing the conservator's salary by 200 pesos a month Burmeister wanted to raise the salary of the porter by 300 pesos a month so that he would not feel degraded in comparison to the other employees. Rather than reduce anyone's salary, Burmeister suggested that appropriations for collections be cut in half.[83] In addition, he offered to sacrifice his own pay raise so that the amount might go instead towards the purchase of materials.[84]

Surprisingly and inexplicably, Burmeister was less successful in increasing the salaries of his staff than in hiring more people to lessen their workload. By 1885 two new posts had been created: zoological assistant and travelling naturalist or collector, the latter position going to the young Spaniard who had served as interim conservator during the early 1880s, Enrique de Carles.[85] By 1892, the year of Burmeister's death, assistants in botany and mineralogy, as well as a vice-director, had been added to the staff.

Even when the Buenos Aires Museum's scientific staff numbered as many as seven, however, Burmeister complained that the La Plata Museum had more than thirty employees, including casual workers. He also contrasted his situation to that of the National Museum of Brazil at Rio, which employed more than twenty staff members occupied with the conservation and augmentation of collections alone. Burmeister also expressed annoyance that the salaries he was able to offer were insufficient to attract well-qualified people.[86]

That salaries were too low is perhaps at least part of the reason why personnel at the Buenos Aires Museum changed frequently, unlike those at the Redpath Museum, who stayed on for years. In Buenos

Aires, a number of men served as inspector at one time or another, including Carlos Berg (brought from the natural history museum at Riga by Burmeister) who used the position to launch a scientific career in Argentina. He eventually became professor of zoology at the University of Buenos Aires and Burmeister's successor at the museum.[87] In the decade between 1866 and 1875, six different men filled the post of conservator. Porters lasted, on average, only a year, although several stayed for no more than a few months. One suspects that Burmeister was quick to find fault with his employees new or old, and that many workers could not tolerate his arrogance and criticism.[88] These frequent changes in personnel further reinforced Burmeister's tendency to run the museum single handed.

CONCLUSION

A Darwinian metaphor may help to summarize the dominant characteristics of the staffing arrangements adopted by colonial natural history museums. The two organizing principles are variation of response and adaptation to local circumstances. Variation appears in the number of salaried employees, which ranged from two to as many as a dozen. The way in which the director used his power also varied from one situation to another, although he always exerted a strong formative influence upon museum development. In some cases, such as that of Burmeister and the Buenos Aires Museum, the director wielded nearly absolute control over museum affairs and united as many functions in his own hands as possible, despite the presence of a large and diverse staff. In other cases, including Dawson and the Redpath Museum, the director learned to delegate authority and welcomed any contribution that lessened his own tasks and responsibilities.

The second characteristic, adaptation, describes this diversity, but it may be employed as well to designate a special attitude towards one's situation. From director to preparators, colonial museum staff were remarkable for their ingenuity and flexibility in responding to local circumstances. Probably it was this adaptability that compelled directors to endure the long physical, emotional, and intellectual journey that brought them to colonial museums in the first place. For the other staff, adaptation meant undertaking a range of tasks beyond those specified, as well as developing more sophisticated skills than those originally required. In consequence, an extraordinary amount of mobility characterized museum service, even at the most menial levels. This remarkable sense of adaptation may also explain why directors stayed at the helm of their museums for such extremely long periods of time, however they might be tossed about and buffeted by changing political winds.

Julius Haast, with friend and moa bones, in his garden in 1867
(Johannes Carl Anderson, *Old Christchurch in Picture and Story*
[Christchurch: Simpson and Williams Ltd., 1949], pl. 88)

Frederick McCoy (Pescott, *Collections of a Century*, facing p. 34)

John William Dawson (Courtesy of the Notman Photographic Archives)

The National Museum of Victoria, *circa* 1865
(Pescott, *Collections of a Century*, frontispiece)

The Canterbury Museum, front view, *circa* 1900
(*Guide to ... Canterbury Museum*, frontispiece)

La Plata Museum (Lydekker, "La Plata Museum," pl. 1)

Exterior of the Peter Redpath Museum, *circa* 1886
(Courtesy of the Notman Photographic Archives)

Burmeister in his office at the Buenos Aires Museum in 1891
(González, *Museo ... de Buenos Aires*, following p. 64)

Construction of Buenos Aires Museum
(Coleman, *Museums in South America*, p. 23)

The Buenos Aires Museum
(González, *Museo ... de Buenos Aires*, following p. 64)

Francisco Moreno (Eduardo Moreno, *Reminiscences*, facing p. 8)

Moreno leading expedition in Patagonia (Moreno, *Reminiscences*, facing p. 216)

New Zealand Room of the Canterbury Museum, showing moa skeletons
(*Guide to ... Canterbury Museum*, facing p. 174)

Interior of the National Museum of Victoria, *circa* 1870
(Pescott, *Collections of a Century*, facing p. 67)

Skeleton of the Black Right-Whale at the rear of the National Museum of Victoria, 1868 (Pescott, *Collections of a Century*, facing p. 66)

CHAPTER THREE

The Founding and Funding of Museums in the Hinterland

A museum is like a living organism; it requires constant and tender care; it must grow or it will perish.

Sir William Henry Flower[1]

Among their diverse duties and tasks, colonial museum builders were usually directly involved in the construction or renovation of their institutions. At the end of the nineteenth century, they joined other museum curators and directors from all over the world in a lively debate about museum design. In the opinion of the Smithsonian Institution's George Brown Goode, following the architect Louis Sullivan's credo, form should follow function. A clear conception of the function of a museum had accordingly to be articulated and sustained from the inception of an institution. Both long-term planning and a steady income — two elusive goals in the colonial context — were essential to Goode's vision. External architecture, he stated, ought to be "simple, dignified and appropriate." Restraint should likewise be exercised in interior embellishment, leaving it "simple and restful." Decoration should not distract the observer from the collections, nor should it reduce the amount of floor or wall space available for display. Each museum should have a reference library, laboratory, storage space, assembly hall, and workshops.[2]

Goode's modest proposals, while in keeping with the austere elegance of the National Museum's expanded quarters, failed to appeal to most of his fellow curators. Many museums in major metropolitan centres such as New York, Paris, and London moved into opulent new buildings toward the end of the nineteenth century. Rich ornamentation, both inside and out, of these Gothic, Romanesque, Baroque, or Classical structures, was the order of the day.[3] High Victorian architecture permitted this wide variety and stylistic eclecticism and "demanded attention by its richness, brashness, ostentation and, where all else failed, sheer bulk."[4] Museum façades announced the content of what lay inside by displaying biological symbolism.

Inspired by these modern cathedrals of science, colonial directors were unlikely to heed a call for simplicity. Such a novel path would not only weaken ties to revered cultural traditions of the home country, but would also seem to diminish the real or imagined power of local dignitaries whose financial or political support was always required. In general, European architectural conventions were modified only to allow for differences in climate, type of building material, or quality of labour available.[5]

According to the *Encyclopedia Britannica*, the architecture of nineteenth-century museums was monumental and imposing, due to their association with national prestige and civic pride. Architects achieved a grandiose effect by incorporating "colonnades and arches, high vaulted interiors, [and] vast flights of stairs" into the new buildings, which were often situated in parks or on broad avenues.[6] This was the age of "unashamed belief in monumentality" that produced the important railway stations of the world. As for museums, standard elements such as towers and arches helped to instill "feelings of admiration, respect and confidence."[7]

Museums in the hinterland usually followed the design of a classical temple, which carried connotations of dignity, antiquity, and permanence.[8] This architectural convention called for a symmetrical façade, a commanding entrance (perhaps with a portico), and a multi-storied central hall surrounded by balconies and staircases.[9] The third edition of James Fergusson's *History of the Modern Styles of Architecture* (1891) singled out Montreal's Peter Redpath Museum as a particularly fine example of neoclassical style emerging from a rather conservative and provincial tradition of British colonial architecture.[10] But the Redpath was out of date; by this time in Britain, the rage for Greek Revival style had been replaced by a new vogue of utilitarian and practical "red brick" buildings.[11]

However out-of-date colonial museums were in architectural style or practice, impressive buildings nevertheless were erected under often inauspicious circumstances in late nineteenth-century Canada, as well as in Australasia and Argentina. The physical appearance of museums depended on the skills of their directors, who had to mobilize resources from often niggardly politicians, legislators, or college trustees. What made their jobs especially taxing was the need to sustain these efforts over a number of years, even decades. Otherwise their early triumphs could too quickly vanish as collections decomposed and buildings deteriorated through neglect.

A unique glimpse of these architectural wonders is supplied by an examination of the letters and diaries of the world-renowned "natural history merchant," Henry Augustus Ward. Our tour of colonial museums will follow that charted by Ward a century ago. He owned perhaps the largest and most important taxidermy firm of the day, in Rochester, NY. A frequent traveller to Europe since his early twenties, by the mid-1870s Ward found that he had exhausted his sources of supply there. He began to undertake ever more extensive and strenous trips, leading his descendant and biographer to call him "a man who often wandered beyond the frontiers of civilization."[12] During the 1880s, Ward travelled to New Zealand, Australia, and South America in order to hawk his specimens and acquire new rarities. The simple love of adventure also stimulated his collecting expeditions. In the course of conducting his business, Ward established long-term correspondences with museum directors like John William Dawson in Montreal and Julius Haast in Christchurch. Ward's long and varied experience with museum curators all over the world makes his remarks especially valuable for unifying and connecting the different situations described here.

CHRISTCHURCH

In the spring and summer of 1881, Henry Ward travelled to the South Pacific. His main purpose in undertaking the long ocean voyage was to set up an exhibit at the international exposition in Melbourne, which would serve to advertise his wares to a new continent. One British competitor feared that as a result of Ward's forays into this market, he himself would be shut out totally thereafter. Ward also used this opportunity to scour exotic markets for new materials such as birds of paradise and proboscis monkeys. Besides stops in Australia and New Zealand, Ward's itinerary included Hawaii, Java, Borneo, Singapore, Siam, Saigon, China, and Japan. Only a recent case of cannibalism in New Guinea dissuaded him from visiting that inhospitable island.[13]

On the way to Australia in March 1881, Ward broke his journey at New Zealand with the intention of meeting his correspondent of some years, Julius Haast. But Haast, unfortunately, had chosen just that time to visit the Melbourne exposition. Although he did not get to meet his long-time friend by mail, Ward did get to see the province of Canterbury's museum in Christchurch, directed by Haast since 1869, after the completion of the first phase of his work on the Geological Survey of Canterbury.[14]

"A soft, wet, green version of Hollywood's Wild West" is the way one writer has recently described early colonial New Zealand. In a low, flat, rather swampy plain at the base of the volcanic Port Hills lay the town of Christchurch. It was the provincial capital, with half the province's population. False fronts and lean-to additions were common, leading one municipal councilor to bemoan what he termed its "Melbournification," or its shoddy, tacky appearance. Drainage and sewage problems brought epidemics every summer in this "city of abominations, grim and menacing to the hardy pioneer and intolerable to the fastidious." Social life displayed drunkenness and immorality all too often for those many early settlers who fancied more refined cultural pursuits.[15]

The turning point for Canterbury province and for Christchurch in particular came during the late 1860s and early 1870s, under the superintendency of William Rolleston. Gold fever had died down and new middle-class immigrants from Germany and Britain were arriving in this town of around 10,000.[16] By the time of this period of especially rapid growth, Christchurch could be described as "a nice, clean, comfortable, well-ordered, square city ... [where] everything is green-looking and English-like." One saw "green hedges, green fields, and lofty green poplar trees, with artesian wells here and there." These developments would have satisfied the Canterbury pilgrims — those Anglican settlers who followed their Oxford-educated leaders to New Zealand in the 1840s — who aimed to replicate at Christchurch the ambience of an English town. Their vision called for developing a pleasing landscape of well-designed gardens, avenues, and buildings, dominated by the cathedral's 240-foot-high spire.[17]

A period of endowing and promoting hospitals, libraries, and educational institutions began, fueled, perhaps, by the disproportionate number of schoolmasters and clergymen among the early colonists.[18] The Christchurch Mechanics' Institute was established in 1860 (becoming in 1868 the Christchurch Literary Institute), followed two years later by a Philosophical Society, eventually called the Philosophical Institute. The society, of which Haast was the prime mover, espoused purely scientific and literary aims, with particular attention to promoting the investigation of local natural history. Church societies such as the Church Institute and the Bible and Christian Knowledge Society aimed to educate the town's adult population. In 1872, a public library was inaugurated, a final transformation of the original mechanics' institute; it was followed, a year later, by the foundation of Canterbury College. By the time that its first Gothic buildings in grey stone were opened in 1877, four professorships had been established, three of which were devoted to the sciences.[19]

Closely associated with the Public Library and Canterbury College was the Canterbury Museum, founded at Christchurch in 1861. Its creation realized a resolution passed two years earlier by the Colonists' Society to establish a natural history museum. The museum's successful foundation so early in the history of the province was due in no small measure to the dynamic leadership and untiring energy of Haast. His collection of between 6,000 and 7,000 geological specimens was lodged in two small rooms in the northeast corner of the Provincial Council Buildings.

Given these unsuitable, cramped premises, the province called for architect's plans for a museum building in 1864, but the council soon allowed the subject to drop. When the topic was reopened four years later, opponents vetoed a grant of £800 for a wooden building on the grounds that fire could threaten the valuable collections. Proponents eventually countered by carrying a grant of £1,200 for a stone building, as well as a small sum for showcases.[20] The new museum quarters on Rolleston Avenue were designed by Christchurch's foremost architect, B.W. Mountfort, who would shortly perfect his technique in the Gothic style by finishing the incomplete cathedral.[21] The town's attachment to Gothic architecture, perhaps rare in the southern hemisphere, was even exhibited in the railroad station, which looked like a succession of chapels at right angles to the platforms.[22]

The Canterbury Museum quickly established an outstanding reputation and came to occupy the largest museum building in the country. Haast himself raised more than one-quarter of the £1,700 initially spent on the edifice through private subscriptions and, in addition, supervised its contruction. But despite his enthusiasm, the absence of long-term planning and stable resources from the beginning meant that the development of the Canterbury Museum was shaped by *ad hoc* arrangements, the precise situation that George Brown Goode had warned against.

The grey stone, lancet-windowed Canterbury Museum opened to the public on a spring day, 1 October 1870. Even today one of the finest buildings in the town, the museum enjoyed a central location next to 500-acre Hagley Park on the winding river Avon, lined with weeping willows. The most impressive display in its main room was a small group of skeletons of the extinct giant moa bird, which ranged in height from 4 feet to nearly 12 feet. Ethnological objects hung from the surrounding gallery, where pictures, geological maps, and specimens of geology and mineralogy were exhibited. At one end of the main room, a small lean-to housed an office and workroom.[23]

At first, Haast claimed that twice the number of specimens contained in the museum could be arranged in the new building. He quickly built up Canterbury's collections by exchanging duplicates with institutions all over the world and by buying from a few dealers like Ward. But soon Haast began to complain that collections were outgrowing exhibition space, leaving him with thousands of birds and insects as well as numerous mammals awaiting display.[24] Haast thereby initiated a vicious circle, a pattern that would characterize the growth of nearly every museum treated here. Empty galleries called for specimens to exhibit. Acquisitions, even if they involved no capital outlay, meant that more space and curatorial care had to be provided. The result — rising costs — increasingly strained the good will of the authorities who had initially promoted the development of museums.

Canterbury's provincial council, at that time supporting the museum's expansion, voted £2,000 early in 1872 to add a two-storey, gabled, Gothic structure at right angles to the original building. What was uppermost in the legislators' minds, however, was the desire to keep costs to a minimum, despite Haast's warning against the short-sightedness of being guided by price alone. Unless display cases were properly built of special timber and made to be airtight, he insisted, they could irreversibly damage the specimens they contained. In the case of the construction of the building itself, clearly the authorities ignored Haast's dictum. The new addition was shortened by 7 feet (to save £160) and a gang of convicts was drafted to lay the foundations.[25]

As a result of further building improvements carried out during the early 1870s, a 50- by 30-foot "moa room" was opened to the left of the museum entrance, along with two smaller lecture rooms on the first and second floors. This development served to differentiate local fauna from foreign collections. Construction also began on detached workrooms where large mammals could be prepared for exhibition.[26] Previously, visitors had complained of "offensive odours" that ruined a stroll through the galleries, coming from nearby taxidermy rooms.[27] By this time, public sentiment could weigh, since around 16,000 signed the guest register each year. The methodical Haast even conducted a study to show that only one in three persons bothered to record his visit, so that actual attendance reached nearly 50,000.[28]

By the mid-1870s, financial restraint replaced the relative generosity that the provincial government had previously shown the museum. To some extent this change reflected the advent of less prosperous times.[29] Perhaps Haast's arguments for the importance of the museum as a counterforce to political centralization were undermined by the abolition of the provincial system in New Zealand. Formerly supportive politicians sneered at the museum, calling it "that consummation of folly — the toy-shop."[30] In addition, management of the museum had passed from its own Board of Trustees to the Board of Governors of Canterbury College (the forerunner of the present University of Canterbury). Although all the former trustees were included in the new board, the existence of a new university probably siphoned off funds from the museum.[31]

An impressive allocation of £14,000 in 1874 was vetoed by a succeeding government the following year, and construction on yet another extension to the original building had to be halted. Thereafter progress on new additions could only be made haphazardly as small grants were received through lawsuits instigated by Haast against provincial authorities.[32] One can only be amazed at Haast's aggressive posture towards state parsimony. Not only did he refuse to accept a reduction in his allocation, but he successfully sued the government for failing to deliver the support it promised.

During this phase of the museum's development, Haast's attention turned to ethnological materials in particular. The museum opened a complete "Maori House" as an exhibition room. Other prehistoric items from Europe and North America were displayed separately. In ethnology, as in natural history, New Zealand and foreign collections were segregated. A second series of additions to the Canterbury Museum were inaugurated in 1878, among them a large mammal room or Great Hall. The former entrance hall was replaced by a skeleton room with both human and animal remains, adjoined by a paleontological room.[33]

By the early 1880s Haast concentrated on further improvements to the museum's metallurgical, technological, and ethnological branches. A somewhat less tightfisted government awarded £2,000 for renovating the Maori House alone. A Technological Hall — at 90 by 48 feet the largest room in the museum — was opened to the public.[34] Henry Ward, visiting the Canterbury Museum at this time, saw the museum during its final expansion. Even these modest accomplishments cost Haast more than a decade's struggle.

MELBOURNE

After spending a month in New Zealand, Ward travelled on to Melbourne via Van Diemen's Land (Tasmania). More than 40 percent of Australia's inhabitants lived in the state of Victoria of which Melbourne was the capital. By this time, Melbourne had been transformed from "a very inferior English town, unpaved, unlighted, muddy, miserable, [and] dangerous" into "a great city, as comfortable, as elegant, as luxurious, as any place out of London or Paris," it was claimed.[35]

No city except San Francisco ever attained such size and importance in so short a period of time as Melbourne. The growth of this "Metropolis of the Southern Hemisphere" owed much to the search for gold, which caused its population to triple in three years during the early 1850s and led to its emergence as the financial and commercial centre of the Australian continent. Melbourne was said to be unsurpassed by any other city in the British colonies in the conveniences of modern life. It displayed fine broad avenues, mansions, and huge warehouses, in addition to a host of churches, banks, theatres, public buildings, and pleasure grounds. To meet the needs of a rapidly growing population (around 150,000 by 1870) public works projects were geared up, resulting in improved railroads, telegraph services, and gas and water supply. Moreover, unlike Sydney and Brisbane, Melbourne had few associations with Australia's history of conscription and penal servitude.[36]

At the international exposition in Melbourne, Ward tended his own display and bought from other participants as well. The size of the exhibition and the Australian government's efficient handling of the whole affair impressed him, in particular its decision to purchase his exhibit. Afterwards he travelled into the bush as far as the Great Victoria Desert.[37]

Before leaving Melbourne, Ward met Frederick McCoy, a commissioner for the exhibition, who directed the National Museum of Victoria in that city. Its impressive title notwithstanding, the museum was supported by the colony of Victoria alone and could not claim to represent the rest of Australia. Nevertheless, the existence of the natural history museum indicated an unusual concern with intellectual matters in Melbourne. The city also had a university and public library, established within twenty years of the town's foundation in 1836.[38] A scientific society and a mechanics' institute had also been created, which, virtually from their inception, boasted respectively a staff of four professors and a membership of nearly 250.[39]

The people responsible for these developments included a generation of administrative officials from the Colonial Office in London, as well as newly arrived professionals — physicians, lawyers, architects, engineers, and surveyors. Scientific life in Melbourne came to be centred on government departments, with meetings held after hours in offices or homes. The institutions established by these scientifically inclined professionals befitted a place that aimed, like Christchurch, to replicate the cultural life of an English provincial town. Indeed, one-fifth of the revenue raised by taxation was expended on educational purposes.[40]

The National Museum, founded in 1854 in the midst of the gold rush, at first had to compete for state funds with a proposed museum of economic geology. Two years later the fledgling natural history museum absorbed the rival institution.[41] By 1854, McCoy, the young Irishman who had come to Victoria as the first professor of natural science at the University of Melbourne, became director of the museum. He would hold this post for the next forty years.

Probably the most infamous act of McCoy's early administration involved his collusion in moving the collections of the museum from two small rooms in the assay section of the Crown Lands Building in Latrobe Street, near the Royal Mint, out to the University of Melbourne, located in what was then a suburb of the city. The Philosophical Institute (later the Royal Society) of Victoria, which had been built up to complement the museum, petitioned various government officials to prevent the transfer of these collections to such a remote location, dubbed "the bush of Carlton" by one historian.[42] McCoy further enflamed his opposition by reading a paper to the society which argued that a museum should provide for serious scientific research and education, rather than offering idle shows for the entertainment of the curious.[43] During the ensuing discussions — which convulsed the Philosophical Institute for several weeks — McCoy quietly moved the specimens himself.

Following McCoy's clever but hotly resented manoeuvre, the government voted £10,000 to construct a suite of four rooms for the museum. These were to be located over the lecture rooms at the university, which was then being built. Despite this physical proximity, McCoy insisted upon "the complete integrity and independence of the collections" from the university. He warned one of his correspondents not to call the National Museum the "University Museum," as "it would be cakes and ale to some opponents of the Museum here."[44]

For a time the new rooms were adequate for the museum's needs and convenient enough to the city (as it turned out) to accommodate 35,000 visitors during 1860 alone.[45] According to one informal survey conducted by McCoy, most museum guests stayed in the galleries for about an hour and one-half. McCoy's survey also led to the surprising conclusion that Chinese visitors numbered in the thousands each year.[46]

As in Haast's case a decade later, McCoy's aggressive acquisitions policy meant that the museum soon began to outgrow its quarters. By the end of 1861, McCoy had petitioned the government on four separate occasions to provide more space for workshops and for materials in the area of economic geology. In June 1862, the government agreed to support the expansion of the museum and supplied the first installment in a series of grants that would eventually total nearly £12,000. The new building, constructed of local honey-coloured brick at the rear of the university grounds, copied the Gothic architecture of Oxford's New Museum. The use of brick made the museum typical of Melbourne buildings of the day, since good stone was rarely available.[47] Inside, rooms for the director, taxidermists, and assayers surrounded a main hall.[48]

It was not in McCoy's nature, however, to be satisfied with what the government had given him. He felt that financial constraints, which had reduced his budget by 30 percent during the late 1860s, interfered with the realization of his plans for the institution.[49] From 1870 on, the museum's annual reports registered concern about inadequate space for exhibiting the collections and demanded a larger structure to ease the crowded conditions. The report of 1879 threatened to restrict acquisitions — an ultimatum that must have amused those accustomed to McCoy's extravagance in this area — unless more room for display was provided. Three years later the annual report pointed out that major accessions had been in the lower divisions of animals, such as insects and fish. These, McCoy sniped, fortunately occupied less space than other classes.[50]

Beginning in the mid-1880s, McCoy began to complain more stridently about crowded conditions in the museum, which, he claimed, were spoiling the system of classification and making display and preservation of specimens increasingly difficult. He may have been especially galled by the fact that other state museums in Australia were at this time receiving unprecedented support and were expanding. The government of Victoria finally began to proceed with building construction during the late 1880s and voted money to this end, but progress was so slow that the collections deteriorated further.[51] To his annual lament about this state of affairs McCoy added, in 1891, a complaint that the taxidermists, in the absence of proper workrooms, were forced to work under unhealthy conditions.[52] He contrasted his straitened circumstances with the Australian Museum in Sydney, whose budget was three times larger.[53] Just for "contingencies" or general expenses, the Australian Museum received more than £2,000 a year as opposed to only £400 for Melbourne.[54]

McCoy's grumblings aside, the 1870s and 1880s were in other respects good years for the National Museum of Victoria. Its record for research improved with the publication of twenty installments of the *Zoology of Victoria* (1870–90) and seven parts of the *Paleontology of Victoria* (1874–82).[55] The museum excelled in popular education at the same time; attendance levels reached new records during the late 1880s, when over 130,000 visitors were admitted each year.[56] The result of these triumphs, unhappily for McCoy, seems to have been only further estrangement and isolation from fellow curators and neighbouring museums in Australia.

MONTREAL

Henry Ward's return from the Far East was not announced in his *Natural Science Bulletin* (the firm's house organ) until January 1882. An outbreak of cholera and smallpox caused his ship to be quarantined and delayed his arrival at San Francisco. Perhaps because his trip to the South Pacific had lasted so long, Ward stayed in Rochester and sent his partner and brother-in-law Edwin Howell to Montreal to set up materials for the opening of McGill University's Peter Redpath Museum. In the July issue of Ward's *Bulletin*, he announced that the firm had supplied skeletons, invertebrates, geological models, fossils, and casts of fossils worth $2,000 to the new museum. The museum's director John William Dawson had toured the Ward and Howell "natural science establishment" less than two years before, in the interests of locating collections for the new museum.[57]

When Edwin Howell visited Montreal, the city had emerged as the commercial and financial capital of Canada in spite of several decades of "periodic tragedies arising from disease, fires, floods, explosion, and sometimes rioting in the streets." As late as 1885, an outbreak of smallpox threatened the predominantly French-speaking city, which then had about 200,000 inhabitants. Yet gradually Montreal began to present a new face; streets were widened, streetcars ran through town, and housing was constructed to serve a growing and wealthier population. The generous use of stone in the central core of the city gave it an air of solidity and a distinctive character. The island city had become a communications centre for Canada, being linked to the outside world by new railroads, telegraph lines, and bridges.[58]

By the time of Confederation in 1867, Montreal had cast off its earlier stigma of being an intellectual desert. Among its cultural bodies, the city possessed two universities: McGill, founded in 1829, and a Montreal division of Quebec City's Laval University, established in 1876. A number of good classical colleges and convent schools attracted serious attention, as well as a range of private and public schools. Both a Mechanics' Institute (1828) and the Institut Canadien (1844) had substantial libraries. Other literary and artistic associations flourished, including the Société Historique de Montréal (1858) and the Art Association of Montreal (1860). The scientific life of Montreal nevertheless was centred around two institutions created in the 1820s, the Natural History Society and McGill University.[59]

Since 1869, Howell's partner Ward had been corresponding with Dawson, whose main responsibility was to act as principal of McGill.[60] When Dawson arrived in Montreal fifteen years earlier, the university museum had consisted of exactly one fossil. Such a deficiency was a serious matter to the Edinburgh-educated paleontologist. At Edinburgh, one measure of Professor Robert Jameson's pre-eminence in natural history had been the collections he amassed over fifty years, collections which served the university and acted as a mecca for scientifically inclined inhabitants for miles around. With the example of his alma mater fresh in his mind, Dawson set out to create a respectable natural history museum at McGill.

In the early 1860s, when the first college buildings were completed, a room was set aside to house such a museum. Slowly the collection grew as a result of purchases made possible by occasional monetary gifts, the fees collected from Dawson's lectures to medical students, and a museum fund established by the banker and brewer William Molson. Important donations of specimens came from other Montreal residents, including Philip Pearsall Carpenter who gave a collection with more than 4,000 species of shells, and the medical practitioner and dean, Andrew Fernando Holmes, who provided a herbarium. Dawson himself gathered fossils and rocks during his summer holidays. Some of these objects were deposited in the museum, while duplicate specimens furnished materials for exchange with other institutions.[61]

In 1862 Dawson boasted that McGill's museum held 10,000 natural history specimens, arranged to illustrate successive lecture topics on that subject. Besides their function as a teaching aid, the collections could be used by local naturalists for research. Yet Dawson was careful to explain that McGill did not intend to amass a "large general collection" to rival those belonging to two other Montreal institutions, the Geological Survey of Canada and the Natural History Society. In fact, Dawson promised that future additions to McGill's holdings would be made in areas not represented in these two museums.[62]

Fifteen years dramatically changed Dawson's view of the purpose of the natural history museum at McGill and its relationship to others in Canada. Foremost in precipitating this change was the Dominion government's decision to transfer the Geological Survey and its museum to Ottawa, the backward national capital. Dawson had maintained almost a proprietary interest in the survey and its museum, lavishing time and effort on improving its collections in paleontology and geology. He felt betrayed by the move to Ottawa and mounted a furious but futile lobby against the plan.

No longer was Dawson content to built a modest museum. He aimed instead to establish "a better collection illustrative of Canadian Geology" than that of the survey in less than a year. Furthermore, McGill professors were "straining every nerve to bring ours up" to the level of a good general museum. What gave conviction to Dawson's determination was an offer from the Montreal industrialist Peter Redpath to provide McGill with a museum building intended to be "the best of its kind in Canada." Redpath's offer — estimated as worth over $100,000 — was the largest gift that McGill had ever received. Besides consoling Dawson for the loss of the survey collections, Redpath wanted to commemorate his twenty-five-year tenure as principal of McGill and, perhaps most important, to dissuade him from accepting a post at Princeton University.[63]

Late in August 1882, the Peter Redpath Museum opened its doors with a reception for 2,000 guests. Dawson called the museum "the greatest gift ever made by a Canadian to the cause of natural science, and … the noblest building dedicated to that end in the Dominion." Journalists acclaimed the museum as "one of the greatest architectural beauties of Montreal," praising "its simplicity of outline and marked constructive strength." The Grecian exterior, built of limestone quarried near Montreal, was conventional, but its proportions were good and the interior layout was well designed, with adequate space to display a series of natural history specimens for teaching purposes.[64]

Entering the Redpath Museum, the visitor saw at the back of the ground floor a handsome lecture theatre with seats for 200 students. Rooms closer to the front of the building would soom accommodate a herbarium, reference library, classroom, boardroom, and office. To the right of the entrance, a staircase displaying archaeological objects and large slabs of fossil footprints, led to the main floor or "Great Museum Hall." Henry Ward's imposing cast of the British Museum's *Megatherium* — set up by Howell and a status symbol for new museums — dominated this floor, which displayed palaeontological, mineralogical, and geological specimens. Fossils in the center and along either side were arranged first by age and second by taxonomy. The visitor, then, could view the general order of geological succession or trace any group of animals or plants through several geological formations. The second floor of the museum — the gallery of the great hall — contained zoological material, both representative types and local forms. Invertebrates were stored in table cases, while vertebrates were displayed in upright cases. The basement contained a laboratory for preparing and storing specimens. Dawson, describing the museum to Alexander Agassiz at Harvard's Museum of Comparative Zoology, called it "the first properly organized thing of the kind we have had in Canada."[65]

The primary function of the Redpath Museum was to serve McGill students and faculty, but a variety of educational and professional organizations also used its facilities. The American and British associations for the advancement of science held geological sessions in the lecture theatre and receptions in the Great Hall during their Montreal meetings in the early 1880s. The province of Quebec's Protestant Association of Teachers and the Canadian Society of Civil Engineers also met in the Redpath Museum. There the Ladies' Educational Association of Montreal regularly heard lectures on botany, zoology, and the "geology of Bible Lands." By coupling its utility for the university with an average annual attendance of around 2,000 during its early years, the Redpath Museum could lay claim to being "the foremost educational institution in Canada."[66]

After a promising beginning, the museum quickly found itself in financial difficulties. The distinguished Montrealers who made up the Redpath Museum Committee, which managed the affairs of the institution, laboured under severe monetary constraints. The university paid a small portion of medical students' fees (several hundred dollars per year) in exchange for their use of laboratory facilities in the museum building. On occasion the Board of Governors advanced funds to allow the museum to balance its accounts, but these amounts had to be repaid. Because McGill had agreed to keep up the museum, according to the terms of Peter Redpath's gift, the corporation paid for repairs and improvements while the museum was held responsible for its own general maintenance. Revenue also came from the 25¢ admission charge levied upon all visitors except university staff and students, McGill graduates, school teachers, and clergymen. In addition, the museum received small sums in interest on the various museum funds and from lecture fees paid by the Ladies' Educational Association (about $100 a year).[67]

Perhaps because of their first-hand knowledge of the museum's dire financial situation — it was rarely out of the red — members of the museum committees gave generously of their money as well as of their time. Redpath made an annual grant of $1,000 for maintenance of the museum building; this was continued by his widow, who increased the sum to $1,500 in 1894. In addition, Louisa Molson, wife of Montreal brewery magnate J.H.R. Molson (William Molson's nephew), contributed $2,000 to establish a fund for paying the salary of Thomas Curry, the assistant curator.

From the beginning, lack of funds impeded the museum's development as a research institution. In 1886 Dawson proposed to publish a series of bulletins or memoirs in order to describe and illustrate important specimens in the museum collections. After a short trial in the annual report, the scheme lapsed. Two years later, a monograph called *Notes on Specimens* began publication. But again because of financial difficulties, the series suspended publication after only one number.[68]

Although Dawson had accomplished a great deal in the first decade of the Redpath Museum's existence, funds were not forthcoming to sustain it in its multiple functions. The move of the survey museum to Ottawa had propelled the Redpath Museum into serving not only the university, but also a city, a province, and a nation. Unfortunately it could not meet its original goals, let alone its acquired responsibilities, given the financial climate in which it was forced to operate.

BUENOS AIRES

The North American continent failed to satiate the curiosity of Henry Ward. Perhaps it was all too familiar to someone who never crossed the same country twice if he could help it. Africa lured him away from Rochester in the mid-1880s. Later in the same decade it was Central and South America. Ward sailed from New Orleans to Costa Rica and Panama. From there he proceeded south, stopping in Ecuador, Peru, Bolivia, Chile, Brazil, and Argentina. All the time he searched private collections, public museums, and even village markets for natural history specimens. He found anteaters, condors, and Indian artifacts such as *bolas*. As for museums, he thought that only those of Brazil and Argentina merited attention. He dismissed as poor, ill-kept affairs others in Lima and Montevideo; the same judgment applied to the natural history museum of Santiago which had earlier thrived under the direction of Rudolph Amandus Philippi.[69]

On 27 June 1889, Ward arrived in what he called the "great, flat, dingy city of Buenos Aires." The city (until recently the capital of Argentina's most important province, Buenos Aires) covered six square miles. Next to Rio de Janeiro, it was the largest city in South America, with around one million inhabitants. During the third quarter of the nineteenth century, its population tripled as European immigrants flocked to benefit from abundant and well-paid jobs, easily obtained capital, and lively commerce and industry. The country's extraordinary agricultural wealth had recently begun to result in the funneling of cattle, sheep, and grain through this port city to the outside world.

By the latter half of the nineteenth century, work had begun on the sanitary improvement of Buenos Aires, but the death rate still exceeded that of similar cities elsewhere, even in non-epidemic years. The yellow fever epidemic of 1871 killed one in nine inhabitants, a death rate unprecedented in the civilized world. All too few magnificent and spacious boulevards like the Avenida de Mayo ran through the city. With the exception of wealthy neighborhoods like Palermo and Belgrano, the city consisted of narrow and closely built-up streets at right angles to one another. Buenos Aires consequently was not only unhealthy but gave the impression of flatness and dull uniformity.[70]

Ward was less impressed by the city than by an imposing collection of Pampean fossils in the National Museum, which he visited the day after his arrival. Two days later Ward made a return visit to the museum.[71] The Museo Público de Buenos Aires had been created by the government of Bernardino Rivadavia in 1812, the first natural history museum established in South America. Another eleven years elapsed, however, before it actually took form on the second floor of the convent of Santo

Domingo, which faced the largest city market at the corner of Belgrano and Defensa streets. A few years later its holdings included only two quadrupeds, several fish, a few hundred birds and shells, and some 800 insects. Under the dictatorship of Juan Manuel de Rosas (1830–54) and the directorship of the chemist Antonio Demarchi, the institution continued to languish. In one five-year period during this "time of decadence," only about 200 new objects were donated to the museum.[72]

Beginning in the late 1850s, the newly created Asociación de Amigos de la Historia Natural del Plata took charge of the museum and worked to revitalize it. With the institution now under the protection of eminent Argentine citizens, including the naturalist Francisco Muñiz and the publicist Manuel Ricardo Treller, gifts poured in; as a result, the size of the collections doubled in only two years. The rector of the University of Buenos Aires was named president of the association, and in consequence, the museum became closely linked with that institution. The university thereupon provided new accommodations for the museum near the entrance to the campus, in an old building at the corner of Peru and Potosi streets. It acquired four exhibition rooms, including one more than 100 feet long, with space for a laboratory, storage, a library, and private rooms for the director. With the museum's expanded quarters, new materials were acquired, and the old collections in some areas such as mineralogy and paleontology were better classified. The French naturalist Auguste Bravard, founder of the short-lived National Museum in the then Argentine capital Parana, declined the post of director. Another European, Hermann Burmeister, accepted the call to a continent he had viewed with increasing interest since his long visits to Brazil and Argentina during the 1850s.[73]

In February 1862, as the interprovincial civil war ended under the presidency of Bartolomé Mitre, Burmeister was named director of the Museo Público de Buenos Aires, succeeding Santiago Torres. This was at a time when other educational institutions in Argentine were being revitalized by an infusion of foreign scholars and government support. The University of Buenos Aires, founded in 1821, acquired a new rector, Juan María Gutiérrez, who displayed a marked sympathy for expanding university resources in the scientific realm. He organized a department of exact sciences, hired professors from Italy to fill the chairs, and offered science courses beginning in 1866. Among those hired were the mathematicians Bernardino Speluzzi and Emilio Rosetti and the natural historian Pellegrino Strobel. In 1872, a group of science students and university alumni under Rosetti's patronage founded the Sociedad Científica Argentina. The society assembled a magnificent library, organized lectures, and published a journal. An Instituto Geográfico Argentino was created a few years later.[74]

Even outside Buenos Aires, scientific life was stimulated. At the University of Cordoba, recently nationalized in 1854, scientific professorships were established during the late 1860s, and Europeans (in this case, all Germans) came to fill them.[75] Burmeister was charged with the long-distance direction of an autonomous Academia de Ciencias Exactas in Cordoba, whose members taught in the local faculty of physical sciences and who were supposed to carry out official scientific investigations.[76] Important for the natural history of sciences was the creation of the National Museum at Parana in 1854, under the direction of a Belgian, Alfredo de Gatry. He was succeeded by Bravard, a mining engineer and geologist who died in the Mendoza earthquake of 1861.[77] Eventually a university museum was created at Cordoba as well; it aimed to embrace anthropology and paleontology, in addition to zoology.[78] This period of creating museums, scientific societies, and journals, as well as of expanding educational facilities, has been seen as the emergence of modern science in Argentina.[79]

Instead of having his museum subordinated to the university, as originally planned, Burmeister was granted "independent direction" of the museum and allowed to report directly to a provincial government minister. Enjoying, then, considerable autonomy as well as an initial grant of 20,000 pesos, Burmeister transformed the museum into an institution organized according to scientific principles, or, as he said, "arranged in the European manner." When he arrived, the birds had been classified according to colour and size. Sorting out parrots from paintings and pottery, Burmeister divided the museum into three principal sections: art, history, and science, emphasizing natural history. The artistic section, said Burmeister, held not a single painting or sculpture of the first rank. The much more valuable historical section contained such archaeological objects as mummies, coins, and domestic artefacts, as well as recent items, such as war trophies and even Rivadavia's desk. But it was the scientific division, the dominant part of the museum since its foundation, that particularly attracted the attention of Burmeister, himself a paleobotanist.[80]

Burmeister's happy relationship with the government — which provided funds for daily expenses, as well as special appropriations for books, specimens, and building construction — lasted fifteen years. In mid-1876, Burmeister received the first of a series of directives asking him to curtail expenditures. That year, the total budget was reduced by 15 percent or 30,000 pesos. The following year funds were decreased by nearly the same percentage or 20,000 pesos. All domains of museum activity suffered as a result of the first set-back to its heretofore continuous expansion.[81] The museum's journal, the *Anales del Museo Público*, which had been funded by special government monies since its inception in 1864, suspended publication in 1874, not to resume again until 1883. During the meantime, the museum had no official publication to exchange with those of foreign museums or to draw attention to its achievements.[82] Financial restraint thereby impeded the museum's ability to encourage, disseminate, or reward research based upon its collections.

In 1878, a young Argentine naturalist named Eduardo Holmberg wrote an impassioned plea for wider public recognition and greater government support for the museum. He took the reader on a tour of the institution, pointing out how paintings, archaeological objects, minerals, molluscs, and large fossil skeletons were still housed together in the biggest room. Collections in ornithology and entomology were dispersed among several rooms and displayed alongside other kinds of items. Holmberg maintained that to divide the museum into clearly demarcated sections or departments would both improve its scientific utility and increase its comprehensibility for the public. Such reorganization, however, required a major extension to the museum's quarters, which in turn necessitated increased funding.[83]

To Holmberg, lack of government patronage for the museum had undermined its function as a popular educator in a number of subtle and interconnecting ways. Although the museum was open to the public every Sunday, the average citizen did not understand what he was seeing. Visitors could merely look at objects in their cases, since there were no staff on call to explain them. Close examination or comparison with other specimens was impossible. In addition, because the *Anales* had suspended publication, residents of Buenos Aires had to consult foreign works to learn about scientific developments at home. Yet the museum library that contained these publications was closed to the public because it lacked a librarian. Furthermore, the shortage of competent staff meant that the introduction of new attractions for the public — popular lectures, for example — was out of the question.[84]

Underfunding had thus reduced the Buenos Aires Museum to a condition where neither its scholarly nor public aims could be fulfilled. A second government directive to economize, issued in 1881, provoked Burmeister to defend his budget. Expenses could not be curtailed, he argued, due to the continuous augmentation of collections and the increasing cost of scientific books and periodicals. In fact, as a result of the limited funds available to him, Burmeister had spent 25,000 pesos out of his own pocket on the museum during the past year.[85] From this time onward, Burmeister's relationship with the government deteriorated steadily. Special requests were often denied, if they were answered at all.[86] As a result, neither staff nor collections received adequate appropriations.

By the time that Henry Ward saw what he called "Burmeister's Museum," it had fallen into a sad state of neglect. Ward complained of its "wretched quarters" and the poor maintenance of what had been basically good material. Burmeister himself, by then aged 81, still held the reins of power but had antagonized everyone, even his own son, by his irrascible disposition.[87] Only death three years later forced him to release the grip he had kept on the museum for the previous thirty years. Poignantly, this occurred as the result of a blow to the head that he suffered when he fell from the top of a ladder in the museum itself.[88]

LA PLATA

The chief reason for the rupture between Burmeister and the government seems to have been the uncertain political climate of the day. In June 1880 the uneasy alliance between *porteños* (residents of the city of Buenos Aires), provincial authorities, and the national government erupted into violence in the southern part of Buenos Aires. Long-standing differences that had divided these parties were finally resolved when, later in the same year, the national government proclaimed the city a federal district and forced provincial powers to withdraw. Despite the turmoil that these events produced, they benefited a new museum, created in 1882 in the provincial capital at La Plata, 40 miles southwest of Buenos Aires. In order to underscore the political significance of this location, impressive new provincial buildings were erected shortly afterwards, including a Greco-Roman edifice intended to house a natural history museum.

Compared to Buenos Aires, La Plata was impressive; Henry Ward was overwhelmed by its "wide streets, ... shade trees, and splendid ornate buildings." If Buenos Aires was the Chicago of South America, as one observer claimed, La Plata aimed to be its Washington. In place of the narrow and dismal streets of Buenos Aires were avenues double or triple the width, "better paved, better designed, embellished with trees, and properly levelled," over which the fragrance of freesias wafted. During two years, more than £10 million had been spent on building and decorating the town, transforming a swampy tract of wilderness into a magical city of palaces, plazas, and parks. Not only government buildings but theatres, a zoological garden, an astronomical observatory, a university, and a cathedral seemed to sprout overnight. Even with a population of 50,000, however, La Plata still looked deserted, with many houses remaining unoccupied and grass growing up in the streets. Dissatisfied provincial employees refused to leave the vibrant life of Buenos Aires, and instead commuted. The "fiat" city had no staple industries and no real commerce.[89]

Ward caught his first glimpse of "a large, elegant museum building of chaste architecture," set in a park facing the zoological gardens, only a few steps from the observatory, beyond a dense grove of eucalyptus trees. Like other public buildings in La Plata, the grand proportions of the museum were intended to represent the extensiveness of the territory belonging to the province of Buenos Aires. Ward was so impressed with the collections in Argentine ethnology, archaeology, paleontology, and zoology that he made three excursions to La Plata during his eight-day stay in Buenos Aires. He returned to the museum at the end of July and twice again during August.[90]

The Museo General de La Plata, founded in 1884 and opened to visitors (though not finished) in 1887, owed much to the Buenos Aires Museum. Its future director, Francisco Moreno, was so impressed by his visits to the Buenos Aires institution and by a childhood meeting with Burmeister that he spent his youth collecting anthropological, archaeological, and natural history specimens, which he exhibited in his home. His enthusiasm for these pursuits earned him the nickname "Fossil."[91] Aided by two brothers in his quest for objects, Moreno won praise from Burmeister himself for the quality of his specimens, as well as from European savants like Pierre Paul Broca, Jean-Louis-Armand de Quatrefages, and Rudolf Carl Virchow. By 1873 Moreno's collection contained more than 15,000 items. Four years later Moreno donated his museum to the province, and it became known as the Museo Antropológico y Arqueológico de Buenos Aires. In 1878, it opened to the public and Moreno was appointed director with a salary of 5,000 pesos a month.[92]

When provincial institutions were transferred from Buenos Aires to La Plata in 1884, it was decided, over some opposition, not to move Burmeister's museum. The decision was made because of the museum's importance to the city's general population and the great risk posed to its fragile paleontological specimens. With the exception of some collections of special interest to the province that were shipped to La Plata, provincial authorities ceded the Buenos Aires Museum to the Argentine nation. Moreno, for his part, was delighted to have his more modest holdings transferred to La Plata where they would serve as the basis of a new provincial museum.[93]

The transfer of the Buenos Aires Museum from provincial to national authority resulted in severe budget cuts. For Moreno, in contrast, the province's relocation at La Plata proved to be just the event he had been hoping for. During his European travels in the early 1880s, he had been profoundly impressed by the great museums of Europe. By moving his anthropological materials to La Plata where they would not have to compete with the Buenos Aires Museum, Moreno could expand them to include all realms of natural history. This development transformed his collections into the cornerstone of a natural science museum of the first rank.[94] It also allowed Moreno to model the museum after the Smithsonian Institution, and to bestow an aura of official, national importance upon the scientific investigations prosecuted at the fledgling institution.[95]

Especially important for the La Plata Museum's future was the enthusiastic support of the provincial governor, Carlos D'Amico. The chronology shows the importance attached to this undertaking in a part of the world where things usually moved slowly: on 4 September 1884 the Buenos Aires museum was transferred to the federal government; on 17 September the La Plata Museum was created; and in October the foundations of the new building were begun.[96] As Moreno described the situation to George Brown Goode, "In my country activity is not [the] rule in official establishments. The La Plata Museum is an exception and people is [sic] astonished."[97]

With his collections housed in temporary quarters at La Plata, Moreno supervised construction of the new museum for the next five years. It was a three-story oval building, with exterior dimensions of 446 by 231 feet, designed by the Swedish and German architects Aberg and Heynemann. Motifs taken from Mayan, Aztec, and Inca ruins decorated the structure inside and out. Guarding the entrance were the museum's "lions" (actually colossal replicas of the extinct Pampean tiger or *Smilodon*) which were posed at both sides of the main exterior staircase. Moreno had planned to place seventy-four busts of famous naturalists in the spaces between pillars all around the edifice. The legislature, however, found this plan excessive and reduced the number to the twelve that still grace the front portico of the building. The end result was not unlike the local railway station, itself "a staggeringly ornate pentagonal building covered in statuary and surrounded [sic] by a dome."[98]

Once inside the museum, the visitor first entered a rotunda surmounted by a glazed dome and surrounded by a circular gallery on the second floor. Large paintings on the rotunda walls, executed by imported German and French artists, showed prehistoric man in the New World, the customs of Pampean Indians, and landscapes of the Andes. The second floor of the museum housed the library and art galleries, while the basement contained laboratories. To soften and complement the imposing structure, Moreno planned a zoological and botanical park around it. The building's cost of 300,000 pesos was about twenty times the price of the nearby astronomical observatory and made the museum one of the most expensive of the impressive new provincial buildings.[99]

Moreno supervised every aspect of the museum's organization in addition to overseeing its construction. Collections were arranged and exhibited so that visitors (who numbered around 50,000 a year during the late 1880s) advanced through the evolutionary history of the earth and life on earth.[100] Thirteen large rooms forming the perimeter of the museum displayed Argentine fauna, both fossil and recent, in what Moreno called a "phylogenetic gallery." The central space treated the physical and cultural evolution of man.

Moreno bemoaned the fact that his attention to the collections, along with a shortage of personnel, prevented the publication of museum guidebooks and catalogues.[101] As Tables 1 and 2 indicate, however, the La Plata Museum had nearly double the budget of the Buenos Aires Museum, and it assembled one of the largest museum staffs anywhere. Indeed, by 1890 the La Plata Museum could print its own official publications, the *Revista del Museo de La Plata* and the *Anales del Museo de La Plata*, in its own workshops.

FINANCES

For Moreno, as for other colonial directors, resources never quite matched expectations. Yet the La Plata Museum was in fact better endowed than the other museums described here. It cost about twice as much as the Peter Redpath Museum and four times as much as the National Museum of Victoria (see Table 3). The greater cost allowed the construction of a larger building, which occupied approximately 32,400 square feet.[102] Its size and price placed it on a par with the National Museum in Washington, DC, which covered more than two acres and cost taxpayers $250,000.[103] At the other extreme, Table 3 shows that the cost of the Canterbury Museum was remarkably low, but this figure is somewhat deceptive. The original building, though inexpensive, was so inadequate that new additions were called for continuously during its first decade, at further cost to the public.

By world standards, the sums expended on new museum buildings in the hinterland (from around £4,000 to £60,000) were both reasonable and respectable. Table 3 also suggests that building a museum became an ever more expensive undertaking as the century progressed. In other words, except in the case of the Canterbury Museum, the available figures suggest that construction costs escalated rapidly as museum creation approached the end of the century. Plotting the date of museum foundation against expenses would create a nearly exponential curve.

Table 2 (p. 37) has shown museum budgets or expenditures. There is some disparity, from the La Plata Museum and the National Museum of Victoria, with several thousand pounds at their disposal each year, to

Table 3
Statistics on New Museum Buildings

Museum	Approximate Date	Cost	Cost (£)	Dimensions (feet)
Canterbury	1870	£3,700	3,700	70 x 35[1]
National Museum of Victoria	1860	£11,700	11,700	150 x 60[2]
Peter Redpath	1880	$140,000[3]	28,000	132 x 72
Buenos Aires	—	—	—	100 long[2]
La Plata	1885	300,000 silver pesos	60,000	446 x 231[4]

[1] Main hall; later enlarged to 90 x 45 ft.
[2] Main hall
[3] Includes fittings
[4] Central part; 70,000 ft^3

Sources: R.T.M. Pescott, *Collections of a Century: The History of the First Hundred Years of the National Museum of Victoria* (Melbourne: National Museum of Victoria 1954), 54; *Report of the Committee of the Public Library to the Trustees of the Public Library, Museums, and National Gallery of Victoria, of the Proceedings of the Institution from the Year 1853 to the Year 1869, and for the Year 1870–1* (Melbourne: n.p. 1871), 52; H.F. von Haast, *The Life and Times of Sir Julius von Haast* (Wellington: Avery Press 1948), 595, 601–2, 628, 819; "The Late Peter Redpath," Montreal *Gazette*, 7 Nov. 1894; JWD, box 37, "McGill University. The New Redpath Museum," newspaper clipping, 21 Sept. 1880; Eduardo Holmberg, "El Museo de Buenos Aires," *El Naturalisto Argentino* 1 (1878): 36; Universidad Nacional de La Plata, *Obra del centenario del Museo de La Plata* (La Plata: Facultad de Ciencias Naturales y Museo 1977), vol. 1, *Reseña Historica*, 3–14; F. Moreno, "Breva reseña de los progresos del Museo La Plata durante el segundo semestre de 1888," *Boletin del Museo La Plata* (1889): 12. For currency conversion, see *The Stateman's Year-book: Statistical and Historical Annual of the States of the World* (New York: St. Martin's Press, 1865–   ). One silver peso = approx. $1 Cdn = approx. 4s British.

the Peter Redpath Museum, with never as much as $2,000 (£400) to spend annually. If one ignores for the moment this variation and estimates their average yearly budgets at around £1,500, colonial institutions fared well from an international standpoint. Although major national museums such as those in Paris and London spent more than £40,000 a year at about this time, the budget of a first-class museum in Britain (outside London) was not even £1,000.[104] Colonial museums were generally supported by provincial or state governments, not national ones, and therefore should be placed among this second rank of museums. According to this perspective, then, colonial institutions were financially better off than their European analogues. The more limited resources of the Peter Redpath Museum are understandable given its status as a university museum operating without government patronage of any kind.

Another unifying feature of colonial museums is their continual complaint about insufficient funding. Periodically, curators found it necessary to advance money out of their own pockets in order to weather short-term liquidity crises. Table 2 shows that in every case, after an initial period of expanding resources, budgets contracted. Directors' perceptions of inadequate and even shrinking revenues, therefore, were grounded in reality.

Further exacerbating the problems produced by diminishing resources, colonial museum curators were frustrated in their desire to direct their own institutions. Whether supported by national governments, provincial governments, or universities, museums owed their continued existence to decisions made by external bodies. Locked in battle with legislators or trustees, directors longed to control their museums' destinies or, at least, to gain a measure of autonomy. As we have seen, this problem affected staffing as it would acquisitions. It also helps to explain why the mechanisms for museum administration were altered everywhere in the hinterland by the end of the century.

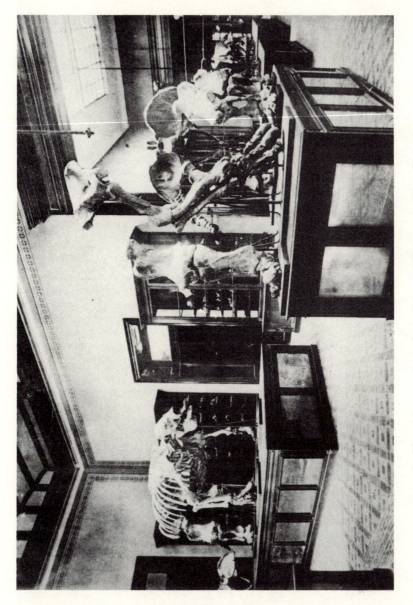

La Plata Museum: *Megatheria* (Moreno, "Museo La Plata," pl. 5)

Interior of Canterbury Museum, *circa* 1870 (Haast, *Life of Haast*, pl. 19)

View of Ward's *Megatherium* cast in the Peter Redpath Museum, *circa* 1885
(Courtesy of the Notman Photographic Archives)

Interior, Peter Redpath Museum (Courtesy of the Notman Photographic Archives)

Reception for the American Association for the Advancement of Science in the new Redpath Museum, 1882 (*The Canadian Illustrated News*, 2 September 1882)

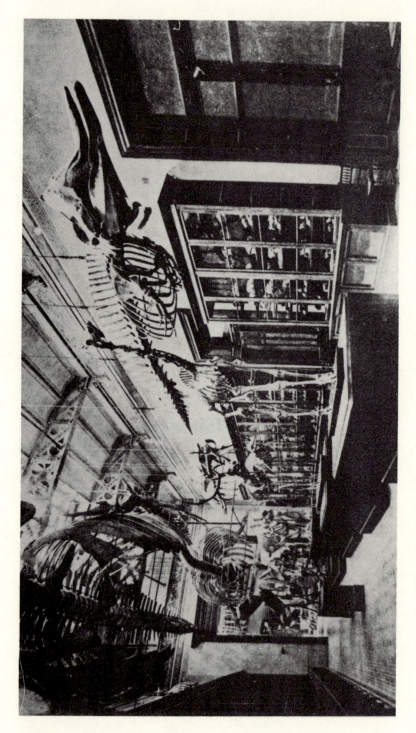

La Plata Museum, Department of Comparative Anatomy (Moreno, "Museo La Plata," pl. 6)

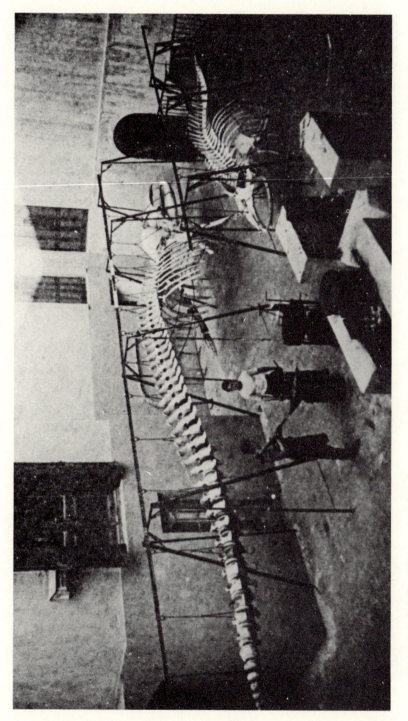

Workshops, La Plata Museum (Moreno, "Museo La Plata," pl. 8)

Vestibule, La Plata Museum (Moreno, "Museo La Plata," pl. 3)

CHAPTER FOUR

Collections

A finished museum is a dead museum, and a dead museum is a useless museum.

George Brown Goode[1]

Distinguished staff, impressive façades, and appealing interior design all helped to make a positive first impression on museum visitors, whether local people, foreign naturalists, or itinerant natural history dealers like Henry Ward. Yet the true measure of the importance of a museum was the overall excellence of its collections. Quantity mattered, of course; major metropolitan museums counted their accessions in the millions. But quantity without quality was meaningless. Without type specimens (which serve to define new species) or other rare treasures, even massive amounts of local materials had little impact at an international level. Linked to the question of the direction of acquisitions, debates ensued over the organization, arrangement, distribution, and classification of materials. Specimens displayed in row upon row bewildered the casual visitor, who learned more from selective displays organized with his or her needs in mind. The scientific observer appreciated museums that provided distinct series for study and display.

Colonial museums, for the most part, neglected to use up-to-date techniques such as explanatory labels and habitat cases. A few institutions adopted the new museum idea and separated research from exhibition collections.[2] Frederick McCoy set out with a master plan to develop teaching collections, based upon the exhibition of generic types and representative geographical groups of species. This "index" to organic life required no later rearrangement, while new specimens could be continuously integrated into the general collection.[3] Making a distinction between local and foreign objects gave other museums some rudimentary arrangement. The remarkable collection of moa skeletons at the Canterbury Museum, for example, strikingly distinguished New Zealand specimens from the other exhibits.[4]

The "collections which fall first into its possession at the time of organization" exerted a major influence upon the character of a museum, according to George Brown Goode.[5] For Montreal's Redpath Museum and the natural history museum at La Plata, the core collections were originally the private natural history cabinets of their first directors, John William Dawson and Francisco Moreno. In New Zealand, the basis of the Canterbury Museum derived from the geological survey of the province under the direction of Julius Haast and Ferdinand Hochstetter. McCoy and the aging Hermann Burmeister were not field workers like their colleagues, and they depended more upon the efforts of collectors exploring the frontiers of their continents to expand the holdings of the Melbourne and Buenos Aires museums. For them, the exchange of regional materials for foreign ones, as well as the ability to purchase wanted specimens outright, was important from the beginning. Yet very quickly the plans of every director required financial support from provincial and national governments or college trustees, although a sufficient level of funding was rarely kept up.

Our museum builders wanted to establish general museums representing the animal, vegetable, and mineral kingdoms, rather than institutions featuring local fauna and flora. To do so, they developed complicated strategies for stretching limited resources to accommodate their grandiose schemes. McCoy blithely ignored financial restraints by purchasing the choicest materials he could get from abroad, and then failing to pay his overseas suppliers for years on end. Less bold were curators like Dawson, who realized that unsolicited gifts of specimens were at best a mixed blessing, and who tried to persuade philanthropists to donate cash instead to be used at the director's own discretion. Haast's style was different; he honed to a fine edge his skills at exchanging specimens, the only way he could obtain the kinds of collections he wanted.

No matter how museum directors obtained materials from the marketplaces of Europe and North America, shipment overseas often had to depend upon the goodwill of sea captains and government agents.[6] But fate could interfere with even the best intentions. Delays in the transmission of letters meant that valuable objects sometimes changed hands before the wishes of museum directors could be communicated. Too often, specimens took years to reach their destinations; on occasion, they were lost forever in shipwrecks. Despite the most careful packing, materials often suffered damage in transit, and fragile objects sometimes arrived smashed to pieces. La Plata's museum director Moreno blamed the "bad manner used in our docks" for the breaking of some zinc-lined cases holding preserved fish; the escaped liquid ruined a shipment of books sent in the same consignment. At nearby Buenos Aires, Burmeister did not know whether to blame the indifference and negligence of customs clerks or a series of fires in Government House for his loss of parcels from the Smithsonian Institution.[7] Only considerable patience, fortitude, and determination allowed naturalists at the outposts of civilization to realize their ambition of amassing collections containing significant materials obtained abroad.

This chapter will describe the general characteristics of the initial collections gathered during the creation of natural history museums in the hinterland, as well as how directors succeeded in improving their holdings. They traded specimens on an open market that was dominated by a few leading dealers in natural history objects. Due to the success of some of these entrepreneurs, even rarities from the colonial environment had begun to turn up more frequently in the marketplaces of England, continental Europe, and the United States than at home. Not only were objects available in greater number and variety, but prices were often lower in metropolitan markets. The skulls and horns of African mammals, for example, available for a few shillings in London, cost as much as £10 in South African curio shops. Colonial museums might benefit from a temporary glut in the market which depressed prices for certain non-native objects. Of course, this process worked the other way round as well and could lower the prices fetched by objects bartered by the colonists.[8]

By the mid-nineteenth century, London had emerged as the center of a flourishing trade in natural history specimens. New commercial ventures reflected the growing popular interest in amassing extensive collections, which drove the prices for bird skins and eggs, insects, and shells higher with each passing year. Advances in the methods of capturing, killing, and preserving specimens, a flourishing maritime trade that penetrated to far corners of the globe, and even postal price reductions and reorganization that eased international transmission of parcels, all contributed to the success of such enterprises.[9]

As natural history became big business, entrepreneurial dealers displaced smaller suppliers and taxidermists. Modest fossil shops such as Mary Anning's in Lyme Regis, a landmark for the gentleman geologist, gave way to more ambitious undertakings. At his shop in the Strand, James Tennant, mineralogist to Queen Victoria, stocked geological maps, hammers, and recent publications, as well as fossils, rocks, minerals, and shells. He also offered courses on practical geology and mineralogy to those willing to pay his guinea-and-a-half fee. Another dealer, George Hoadley King (who moved from Ipswich to Torquay in order to buy up the "seaweed and shells" brought together by a recently deceased supplier) promised to have a boat awaiting visiting naturalists. In London, W. Cutter of Great Russell Street handled skulls and other "ethnological curiosities" and offered to point out "lucrative localities" to gentlemen collectors travelling abroad.[10]

Because the store had to be minded and a multitude of other matters attended to, most clever businessmen began to leave their fieldwork to professional collectors. Whether searching for insects or birds, these collectors knew that the rarest and most aesthetically appealing objects commanded the highest prices in the marketplaces of London or Paris. Even common species of brightly colored butterflies and sparkling minerals without any scientific or intrinsic value attracted buyers. Objects like shells had the added advantage of being durable and easy to handle, conserve, and display.[11]

Conservation and ecology were not yet an issue. Someone like James Gardner of High Holborn could describe himself as a "naturalist" *and* "plumassier and furrier" without contradiction. (Besides selling furs and plumes, he also made artificial eyes). J.A. Brewer (Reigate and London) specialized in the small objects needed for herbaria and insect collections.[12] Traders in butterflies and beetles offered the widest range of goods: apparatus for capture; labels and a variety of clips, hooks, and pins for mounting; cardboard trays and storage cabinets; and glass-topped boxes and display cases. Across the ocean, the Rochester taxidermy firm run by Henry Ward and his brother-in-law Edwin Howell offered a range of products. These included: plaster casts of fossils and skeletons, almost indistinguishable from the originals; Blaschka glass models of invertebrates and plants; and even special natural history cabinets, packaged as teaching aids for colleges and universities. Always diversifying their stock, Ward and Howell soon offered relief maps, prepared microscopic slides, and anatomical models.

Although colonial museums bought from leading dealers and swapped specimens with major European and American institutions, neither money nor goods automatically gave entry into the complicated system by which specimens changed hands. Metropolitan museum keepers often played a vital role as intermediaries, acting in the interest of less fortunate colleagues elsewhere. Since they were on the spot, they could exercise powers of personal persuasion denied to museum builders overseas. Nevertheless, colonial curators themselves possessed a keen sense of how to buy, sell, or trade materials to best advantage.

MELBOURNE

In a paper on museums that he wrote in 1856, just before he was named director of the National Museum, Frederick McCoy differentiated between local and general museums. Local museums, however complete, limited themselves to specimens gleaned from a particular geographical area, while general museums displayed generic types of organisms collected from all over the world.[13] McCoy envisioned the Victoria museum (called "national" out of jealousy of the "Australian" Museum in Sydney) as a general museum devoted to "the exhibition to the public of examples of all the natural products of the earth." He insisted that, in the absence of foreign specimens for comparison, investigators could not hope to identify local materials properly: "As well might you expect to understand the politics of one European state without reference to the acts and laws of the others, as attempt to investigate the natural products of a colony without at least certain typical specimens from all the other parts of the world."[14]

In his desire to impress the observer with variety, McCoy adopted one of British Museum superintendent Richard Owen's maxims of museum exhibition: to display specimens that called attention to an animal group by accentuating a particular quality. A whale skeleton, for example, showed the enormous size attained by aquatic mammals; a specimen of the extinct moa (*Dinornis maximus*) represented the biggest bird ever known to man; a skeleton of the great Irish deer (*Megaceros*) illustrated the largest antlers ever seen.[15] McCoy accordingly placed a 90-foot whale skeleton (also a type specimen) outside the museum, where over the years it became covered with moss. There it didn't threaten to crowd the galleries, and it also provided a novel outdoor exhibit.

McCoy always tried to display his specimens to best effect. Large vertebrates went to the middle of the ground floor, where they were sure to attract attention. For dramatic impact, McCoy also presented some zoological specimens in geographical groups rather than along traditional systematic lines. One observer heartily disliked these staged, theatrical displays, which he dismissed as a "grotesque failure." Indeed, after McCoy's death the regional groupings were dismantled.[16]

Whatever the aesthetic virtues of McCoy's exhibits, he, more than any other colonial director, became a master at purchasing natural history specimens for the National Museum. He spent about £10,000 during the early 1860s, before the state parliament tired of his excessive expenditures and European suppliers wearied of his delayed payments (see Table 4). For half a decade, McCoy brilliantly exploited this system and built the National Museum into a major collection.

Finding a sympathetic collaborator to conduct his affairs overseas was essential to McCoy's success. Yet locating such an agent was not easy. McCoy confided to his mentor, the geologist Adam Sedgwick, that neither Richard Owen nor Roderick Impey Murchison, the Geological Survey director, had answered his request to buy skeletons and mining models "for the Museum I am 'growing' here." He asked that his wish

Table 4
McCoy's Expenditures on Specimens from Major Suppliers

Year	Gray	Walker	Cuming	Geale	Damon	Westwood	Gerrard	Gould[1]	Reeve	Year Total
1857	500	—	—	—	—	500	143	650	—	1,793
1858	276	—	—	—	—	100	—	503	—	879
1859	250	—	—	—	—	—	—	449	—	699
1860	200	—	—	—	—	—	—	370	—	570
1861	623	—	—	—	263	—	178	38	—	1,102
1862	203	100	359	—	274	—	436	360	351	2,083
1863	811	—	242	—	100	—	135	108	122	1,518
1864	319	—	861	—	760	—	322	17	—	2,279
1865	—	26	185	—	647	—	457	224	—	1,539
1866	—	135	—	64	—	—	171	8	—	311
1867	—	—	—	40	—	—	370	170	—	648
1868	—	30	—	24	—	—	—	143	—	197
1869	—	—	—	106	100	—	—	33	—	239
1870	—	—	—	178	100	—	391	—	—	669
1871	—	—	—	—	400	—	—	6	—	406
1872	—	—	—	—	—	—	—	6	—	6
1873	—	41	—	305	—	—	—	9	—	355
1874	—	—	—	306	—	—	149	—	—	455
1875	—	—	—	189	—	—	149	—	—	338
1876	—	—	—	68	—	—	194	—	—	262
1877	—	—	—	78	—	—	25	—	—	103
1878	—	—	—	91	—	—	181	—	—	272
1879	—	—	—	—	58	—	110	—	—	168
Total	3,182	332	1,647	1,449	2,702	600	3,411	3,094	473	

[1] Includes books

Source: NMV, invoice book; Agents General for Crown Colonies, National Museum Account; letter-books 1–4 (1857–78); incoming letters.

for "dried plants, birds, beasts, fishes, insects, etc." be transmitted to Sedgwick's colleagues at Cambridge, the botanists J.S. Henslow and C.C. Babington, who knew "all the entomologists and ornithologists and craniologists and other -ologists so well."[17] Only two old friends at the Geological Survey's Museum of Practical Geology at Jermyn Street in London agreed to help McCoy at this early stage in the development of the Victoria museum. Trenham Reeks handled his financial transactions in the metropolis, while Reeks's associate, John William Salter, procured several fossil collections, including one with 1,200 specimens of British Silurian fossils for £100. Salter also sent McCoy sketches of certain items in the Jermyn Street museum's collections.[18]

Perhaps at the suggestion of his Cambridge or London friends, McCoy asked John Edward Gray, Keeper of Zoology at the British Museum, to find someone "to look out specimens" and "write cata-

Table 5
Some Examples of Specimen Prices

Item	Price (£)	Date
1,400 birds	400	1858
100 species of shells (300 specimens)	50	1858
Elephant skeleton (prepared)	75	1862
Giraffe	22	1862
Crocodile (15 ft.)	15	1862
Lioness	10	1862
Series of South American monkeys	80	1862
Large African rhinoceros	350	1875
Grizzly bear (large male, stuffed)	31	1876
Hippopotamus (mounted)	64	1877
Gorilla (stuffed)	30	1882
Gorilla (skeleton)	30	1882

Source: NMV, letterbooks 1–4 (1857–78); incoming letters; TL, folder 63, Flower to Haast, 13 Dec. 1875; H.F. von Haast, *The Life and Times of Sir Julius von Haast* (Wellington: Avery Press 1948), 782; R. Damon, flyer, 1858 (courtesy of L.B. Holthius, Curator of Crustacea, Rijksmuseum van Natuurlijke Historie, Leiden).

logues" for his museum. He wanted examples of generic types and geographical groups of species, named according to British Museum rules, in order to "get a good general view of Zoology out here." Instead of handling the "tedious matter" over to "one of the zoological assistants," as McCoy had suggested, Gray himself took charge of purchasing what amounted to more than £200 worth of specimens a year during the late 1850s and early 1860s (see Table 4).[19] He also soon became McCoy's financial agent in London, apparently because Reeks's idiosyncratic bookkeeping methods had mystified the National Museum's auditors.

Gray was proud of the bargain struck with Liverpool's Derby Museum, which sold him 128 mounted mammals and 10 skins for just over £140 — less than the usual cost of stuffing alone, he claimed. (See Table 5 for some typical prices of natural history specimens.) It took him six months to have 2,000 species of shells mounted on boards and another three to name and catalogue an assortment of fish and reptiles preserved in alcohol.[20] In 1863, Stevens's auction house put the collections of the late entomologist John Curtis up for sale, and Gray bought £700 worth of insects for McCoy.[21] He had, however, to return a collection of crustacea because he could find no one to identify them. He even offered to travel to France in order to evaluate 8,000 bird specimens offered for £2,400 by the Verreaux taxidermy firm in Paris. When the British Museum received gorilla skins from Paul Du Chaillu in 1866 — they were of superior quality to the famous trio purchased by Dr. Crisp of London three years earlier — Gray gave second choice (after the British Museum) to McCoy, who wanted them badly. Once McCoy began to buy heavily from the taxidermist Edward Gerrard, Sr., Gray's assistant at the Museum and "right hand man," McCoy still asked Gray to approve all shipments.[22] Clearly Gray gave unstintingly of his time and talent to help build the collections of a man he had never met and a museum he would never see.

McCoy's dealings with and dependence upon Gray declined after 1864, almost certainly because Gray suffered a debilitating stroke in that year. By that time, largely as a result of Gray's help, McCoy had obtained the introductions necessary to communicate directly with professional natural history dealers and collectors. Colonial curators recognized that the choicest and least expensive materials, even from their own locality, came from those collectors stationed abroad who made periodic forays into the bush. When McCoy wanted insects from Asia, the Pacific islands, and his own Australia, he contacted British Museum entomologist Francis Walker. He gently urged Walker to exercise his powers of persuasion on Alfred Russel Wallace and some others of "the 1001 collectors known to him" on behalf of the National Museum. For Australian birds, he went directly to John Gould, who had spent years gathering specimens in the outback before returning to London. For shells, McCoy wrote to Hugh Cuming, whose search for exotic materials led him "through sickness, rainy seasons, and all the inconvenience of travelling through unexplored countries by land and sea." Working principally on the Pacific coast of South America and in the South Seas, Cuming harvested over 1,800 species of shells and 1,900 plants in one thirteen-month period. Any serious conchologist had to buy from Cuming, who eventually amassed the largest and most valuable collection of shells ever brought together by one individual.[23]

McCoy began to deal with Cuming in 1862; he wrote that he looked for a box of shells by every steamer. He explained that he wanted the most complete series possible for each genus, including the rarest items, whether Australian or foreign species.[24] Accounts show that he purchased more than £800 worth of shells from Cuming in a single year (see Table 4). Such a customer — especially one who begged to "let no specimens escape" him — would not be neglected by Cuming's secretary and successor in the business, Robert F. Geale. For nearly a decade Geale forwarded shells on a regular basis, despite McCoy's failure to settle his bills or to return unwanted specimens promptly. When McCoy kept shells for three years or longer before returning them, Geale complained that he was being forced to take a loss on specimens that had since become common. Without capital, he pleaded, he couldn't buy objects as they came on the market. But not until 1878 did Geale suggest ending their agreement, and then with the excuse that McCoy's collection had become so rich that there were few gaps left for him to fill.[25] In fact, Geale probably tired of McCoy's perpetually late payments.

Next to the collector himself, prime specimens came from those leading dealers who underwrote expeditions or who purchased from museums and amateurs renowned for extensive and highly specialized collections. Henry Ward's travels through South America, Australia, and New Zealand allowed him both to tap local sources of natural history materials and to find new customers such as McCoy for his wares. McCoy even bought Australasian specimens from Ward, as he did from the London natural history publisher and supplier of shells, Lovell Reeve.

McCoy tried to persuade Reeve to cooperate with the collector Hugh Cuming in order to avoid duplications in his shipments, but such an arrangement was out of the question in the jealous world of natural history dealing. Reeve called Cuming's wares nothing but "showy things" and the "duplicates and ordinary incoming specimens of a dealer's stock." He urged McCoy to purchase instead from a collection in his possession assembled by William Metcalfe. Unlike Cuming's specimens of sometimes uncertain provenance, each item in this collection carried original tickets and had intrinsic scientific value.[26]

In the end, Reeve sent McCoy species in which Cuming was poorly stocked and avoided Cuming's great strength, land shells. He explained that Australian shells, especially sea shells, were always dear; one shell collected by the *Beagle* had sold for £40 twenty years before. Since McCoy had asked for particularly rare items, Reeve selected over 1,000 packets of shells for him from the Metcalfe collection. The final bill ran to more than £300. Despite McCoy's large purchases, Reeve soon became disenchanted with his Australian customer. He complained of the trouble in supplying species from a restricted locality and about the time it took to examine, name, and send them to Melbourne on approval. It was particularly galling that McCoy had ceased to correspond since 1862 yet still owed Reeve more than £200 two years later. Reeve, who had by this time given up dealing in specimens altogether, threatened to take legal action against McCoy through the Colonial Secretary. At Reeve's death in 1865, McCoy still owed at least £80.[27]

During the early 1860s, McCoy bought what was at the time a complete series of British shells and plaster casts of fossils from yet another supplier, Robert Damon of Weymouth. McCoy was especially interested in purchasing a series of "oolitic fossil plants" (from the Jurassic formation, according to modern geological terminology) from Yorkshire; he wanted to compare them with those of Victoria. After denouncing Damon's collector as "neither energetic nor agreeable," McCoy managed to persuade Damon himself to travel to Scarborough on his behalf in order to convince several gentlemen there "to resign their best specimens." Damon's ability to "step beyond his usual course, and use every possible local and personal exertion" obtained John Lycett's notable collection for McCoy for £200.

Given the demands McCoy made of Damon — including his continual nagging to send authentic and high-quality specimens, properly prepared, packed, and fully insured — McCoy's three-year delay in paying seems to be the ultimate affront. Yet in 1875, Damon still had to beg McCoy not to return, at that late date, some of the oolitic fossils McCoy had kept for the past twelve years. Part of the balance owed Damon was not paid off until 1876, because of what McCoy called a series of political contests in Victoria that involved the museum. McCoy was referring to the fact that the trustees who oversaw the museum were no longer willing to support his excessive and repeated expenditures.[28]

Skeletons and skins of large mammals came to Melbourne from Gray's assistant at the British Museum, Edward Gerrard, Sr., whose London taxidermy firm (run with his son, Edward, Jr.) specialized in these items.[29] McCoy was especially keen to acquire gorilla skins, due to the popular appeal of these animals.[30] Public appetite, already whetted by hints from the evolutionists of man's descent from the ape, was further stimulated by Paul Du Chaillu's tales of gorilla behavior in equatorial Africa and the controversy that he caused in London scientific circles.[31] McCoy thought that acquiring one of Du Chaillu's gorilla skins on the auction block at Stevens's in 1863 would be the most effective means of channelling popular enthusiasm into support for his museum. Although Gerrard and Gray eventually persuaded him that the skins were less than perfect, McCoy tried to convince the eventual purchaser, Dr. Crisp of London, to give them to what he poignantly called "a Museum in such an unfavourable position as this."[32]

McCoy impressed upon the elder Gerrard that he should send only the finest specimens, such as those from animals that had died recently in London menageries and zoos. Records show that Gerrard forwarded all manner of things: an elephant skeleton, a rhinoceros head, a stuffed and mounted hippopotamus, deer, giraffes, monkeys, crocodiles, lions, and antelopes. Gerrard also prepared specimens, even skeletons of animals from Victoria which McCoy sent to him for proper mounting. McCoy asked that all mammals — including huge specimens like elephants and whales — be stuffed right away or "while green," since taxidermic skills were in short supply in Melbourne and large objects could not be prepared at all there. This procedure also minimized damage when specimens travelled through the heat and humidity of the tropics. By 1864, McCoy had found a local taxidermist who could mount big mammals, but he still needed to have artificial eyes shipped from London.[33] As late as 1885, however, McCoy continued to order fully prepared North American mammals from Henry Ward because of the remarkable quality of his firm's work.[34]

Few colonial curators could match the combination of calculated entreaties, gentle insults, and outright bluff that permitted McCoy to string along his suppliers (who were often his creditors) for years on end. More typical, perhaps, was Montreal's J. W. Dawson, who timidly suggested to Henry Ward (from whom he had purchased over $2,000 worth of specimens) that he give a discount for prompt payment.[35] McCoy nonetheless did pay thousands of pounds for specimens from a number of natural history dealers, and this gave him a modicum of power in business dealings (see Table 4).

This situation changed dramatically during the mid-1860s, when government auditors refused to allow McCoy's imaginative bookkeeping to continue. At this point, he turned to the exchange of duplicate specimens in order to procure additional items for the museum. McCoy sent off thousands of objects to governments, museums, and learned societies all over the world.[36] Eventually he wearied of this tactic, perhaps because foreign institutions did not reciprocate to his satisfaction.

McCoy's activities fell under the jurisdiction of various government bodies, since political structures in Victoria were frequently reshuffled during this time. The authorities were always tightfisted towards the museum, but McCoy never ceased to bicker, wheedle, and badger them for more. Political and financial ambiguities were finally resolved, but to his detriment, when the museum was placed under the management of fifteen trustees in 1869. In the next year, the National Museum's mining and agricultural exhibits were transferred to a new competitor, the Industrial and Technological Museum. This action undercut McCoy's commitment to display the natural sciences in their totality along with their applications, and it reduced the museum's purview to natural history alone. In addition, the trustees cancelled some of McCoy's contracts overseas, fired a number of his staff, and tried to change his title from director to curator.[37]

With the passage of time, however, the trustees wearied of their personal vendetta against McCoy. By 1877 he was allowed once again to place orders with suppliers overseas. A decade later the collections were valued at nearly £50,000 and the museum had earned a reputation as one of the finest in the southern hemisphere. Even a potentially devastating fire in the museum was contained and insurance paid for the limited damage.[38] In the mid-1890s a financial depression and consequent budget cuts virtually stopped the purchase of new materials and forced McCoy to look for specimens among the corpses at the local Zoological Gardens.[39] Nevertheless, by 1900 the museum could claim more than 500,000 specimens.[40]

CHRISTCHURCH

What McCoy accomplished by purchase, Julius Haast achieved chiefly by exchange. Even before the province of Canterbury decided to establish a museum, Haast had been busy swapping specimens with foreign institutions and collecting valuable New Zealand materials during his geological survey of the countryside. By 1864 he had acquired 6,000 natural history specimens in this fashion.[41] All this activity pertained to just one of the museum's departments, since coins, medals, and works of art were exhibited alongside natural history and ethnological materials. Not surprisingly, given his background in geology, the scientific departments interested the director the most.

In the realm of natural history, Haast tried to present a selective exhibit of specimens derived from both foreign and local sources. The only mammals and birds displayed, for example, were those that either represented a genus or showed remarkable beauty, form, or color. Haast, like McCoy, was especially interested in obtaining type specimens identified by authorities abroad. He did this, he claimed, in order to make the museum educational and more than "a collection of curiosities." A preponderance of foreign material would have the added benefit of increasing the museum's prestige by any standard — local, national, or international. As a result of Haast's scientific concerns, the number of foreign items came vastly to exceed that of New Zealand flora and fauna.[42] Local materials were reserved for special exhibits, while the general collections were arranged systematically or stored in accessible drawers. Haast also planned instructive displays of New Zealand wool, timber, and building stone.[43]

When the Canterbury Museum opened its doors in 1870, it possessed more than 25,000 specimens, roughly one-third of which remained in storage.[44] Haast promised to display quadrupeds and birds just as soon as showcases were provided. A cabinet to arrange native and foreign insects had been ordered from England. Also on their way from Europe were a handsomely mounted lion, a panther, a leopard, and a gorilla that would "form an ornament to any Museum," Haast claimed. At that time there were no facilities to show specimens of New Zealand botany, geology, or paleontology.[45]

Very quickly, however, Haast's "embryo museum" came to depend for its development upon moa bones, collected locally, and on the exchange materials they brought. Moas were prime objects for bartering purposes, since, as one observer put it, "what Niagara is to ordinary waterfalls, the Moa was to all the bird-tribe." Periodically from the mid-1860s onward, huge assortments of moa bones and of artefacts of the aboriginal tribes that had hunted the extinct birds were crated up from sites near Christchurch. In 1866, a deposit was discovered at Glenmark Station swamp, in hilly country fifty miles north of the town; in Haast's opinion it contained the remains of at least 1,000 moas. This excavation produced enough exhumed bones to fill a large four-horse wagon and provided the first seven complete skeletons for the Canterbury Museum. Upon seeing photographs of the exhibit of these extinct creatures, the finest moa collection in the world, Darwin expressed his astonishment. Alexander Agassiz of the Museum of Comparative Zoology remarked that "a single room like that is enough to make all the museums of the world jealous of you."[46] A second discovery two years later permitted exchanges with foreign museums and meant that for the first time moa bones were displayed in locations abroad other than England.[47]

Haast fell easily into the role of a "merchant in Moas and Mammals" because of his earlier experience as a dealer in mineralogical specimens, perhaps with August Krantz's firm in Bonn.[48] How well he performed the task is revealed in his correspondence with the stormy Richard Owen, who had first written to Haast to obtain a moa skeleton for the British Museum. Owen really wanted the specimen for his own personal research on the huge extinct bird. He offered to send plaster casts of objects in the British Museum in exchange.[49]

Haast expected more than this for the moa skeleton that he shipped to Owen nearly five years later. Similar skeletons generally fetched £20 to £40, depending upon their size, age, quality, and completeness.[50] Not only was Haast uninterested in casts — which might be exchanged only for casts, according to the rules of the Canterbury Museum — but he wanted a few rare objects rather than a quantity of common material. Haast sought specimens of large mammals and birds in particular rather than the *Megatherium* cast that Owen proposed to send.[51]

Owen seems to have assumed that Haast would continue to support the British Museum, despite his own disinclination to meet Haast's specific requests. He forgot that, although the Austrian Haast headed a museum in a British colony, his continental background provided him with an extensive network of correspondents in Europe. Owen was therefore shocked to discover in the *Comptes rendus* of the French

Académie des sciences that Alphonse Milne-Edwards at the Paris natural history museum had received an impressive collection of moa skeletons from Haast. Milne-Edwards, like Owen, had developed a keen interest in the extinct birds, but he was wise enough to send many of the objects on Haast's shopping list. He also flattered Haast by suggesting that he might be appointed a foreign member of the Académie des sciences whenever a vacancy occurred. By this time, the British Museum was still in Haast's debt for the earlier skeleton, and Haast repeated his request for duplicate specimens despite Owen's insistence that the desired materials were not kept on hand there. As Haast summed up his view of the matter, "a *poor* provincial Museum has acted very hand-somely towards an Institution which has about [one] hundred times the income of it."[52]

Richard Owen's pettiness and selfishness were legendary, but even less greedy men were often unwilling to engage in trafficking in speci-mens. Neither Alexander Agassiz at Harvard nor Albert Günther, Gray's successor as Keeper of Zoology at the British Museum, was interested in trading duplicates for New Zealand rarities.[53] William Henry Flower, at the time the curator of the museum of the Royal Col-lege of Surgeons and Owen's eventual successor at the British Museum, was more sympathetic. Flower acted as Haast's London agent, parlaying moa bones and archaeological remains into new collections for the Can-terbury Museum. Usually Flower sold Haast's rarities to the British Museum, but in one case he persuaded a patron to buy a moa skeleton for £50 and to present it to Flower's own museum at the College of Surgeons.[54] With cash in hand, Flower then got what Haast wanted from local dealers in natural history specimens. Finally, he carefully prepared, packed, and insured these objects, before sending them on their way to Christchurch.

Flower tried to accommodate Haast's every desire, as Gray tried for McCoy. He forwarded skeletons of a python, codfish, deer, and ostrich (the latter to be used both as a model for articulation and for structural comparison with the moa). By the early 1870s, Flower had sent mounted skins and skeletons of large mammals such as gorillas, giraffes, and elephants. These were obtained through Edward Gerrard, Sr., whom Flower called "the best natural history agent in London." An order more difficult to fill was Haast's surprising request for a preserved head of a New Zealand Maori, which Flower coaxed away from the curator of the Brighton Museum.[55] Only after Haast astonished Flower with the request to spend £700 on specimens in 1873 did Flower finally tire of sacrificing precious research time in order to attend to Haast's demands.[56]

In general, Haast depended mainly upon barter to build up the collections of the Canterbury Museum. However, the disappointing results
of his transactions with natural history dealers show how poorly the
exchange system worked, in contrast to what McCoy achieved by
purchase. Robert Damon began exchanging specimens with Haast
about a decade after he had first supplied McCoy, in the hopes of obtaining New Zealand sea shells. Haast, on the other hand, wanted
Damon to sell moa bones for him. This arrangement was somewhat
less satisfactory than both parties envisioned at first. Damon warned
Haast that he found few customers for such items, even when asking
only £5 for a set of leg bones. He explained to Haast that, contrary to
what one might expect, such specimens were often worth more where
they were found than elsewhere. Seven years later, only one pair had
been sold. Furthermore, Damon insisted on selling some of his own
wares for cash only.[57]

Around 1880 Haast tried to set up an exchange arrangement with
Edward Gerrard, like that with Damon, but again he found an unen-
thusiastic response to his New Zealand rarities. The market was glutted
with kiwi (*Apteryx*) skins and skeletons, wrote Gerrard, and he could
pay only £1 apiece. Haast's only option was to wait for a few years to
see if the situation might improve.[58] In the meantime, Haast tested the
waters of the North American market through his friend Henry Ward.
There too he found that museums and collectors had been flooded with
moa bones of all shapes and sizes.[59] Haast's experiences show the constraints imposed by the exchange system. Working without the flexibility of cash in hand, he was a captive of the marketplace. He could not
buy unless he sold. Nor could he always sell when his own materials
commanded the highest prices or buy to take advantage of unexpected
bargains.

Although Haast may not have managed to trade duplicate specimens
with the finest museums and the most aggressive dealers, he could
count nearly thirty institutions in Europe, Asia, Africa, Australia, and
North and South America among his collaborators. The Buenos Aires
Museum, for example, swapped rhea skins for moa bones. In addition,
Haast managed to persuade New Zealand shipping companies to carry
these materials free of charge.[60] The collections received in return, as he
bragged in the early 1870s, would "form an ornament to any museum
in the Home country, however extensive and long established."[61] The
more than 25,000 specimens belonging to the Canterbury Museum
were worth over £10,000 and included many irreplaceable items. By
1873, the museum's holdings had increased to 56,000 specimens, nearly
half of them zoological.[62]

MONTREAL

To a lesser extent than Haast, John William Dawson made use of the exchange system to build up the collections of the Peter Redpath Museum. He also on occasion purchased materials, but severely limited resources made him especially dependent upon donations from local supporters. Indeed, his own cabinet of nearly 10,000 Canadian rocks and fossils (valued at $5,000) formed the nucleus of the museum's holdings. The heirs of William Logan, as part of a complicated manoeuvre related to the transfer of the Geological Survey to Ottawa, donated $4,000 to form a collection in memory of the first director of the Canadian survey. With these funds Logan's former assistant, James Richardson, was employed to collect duplicates of Canadian specimens held exclusively by the survey museum. Dawson maintained that exhibits of these materials would stimulate the discovery and exploitation of Canada's natural resources. In addition, "well-arranged collections of natural objects" were the best means of impressing the "power and divinity of Nature's author" upon the mind.[63] Redpath himself chided Dawson for his insatiable appetite for "stones and bones and skeletons of all kinds" that might overwhelm the new building.[64]

Another important helper in Dawson's activities was his son, who worked for the Geological Survey of Canada. In the summer of 1882, George Mercer Dawson toured Europe, sent home information about continental museums, and cultivated useful contacts abroad. Particularly impressed by the provincial museums of France, George urged his father to add "a small typical local collection" to the Montreal museum, "with map to accompany it so that anyone could go to the precise spot at which points of importance exist." At Bonn, he visited the geological "merchant" August Krantz, whose immense collection furnished much less expensive specimens than those obtained in London. George found that he could buy rocks and minerals in the French countryside for as little as 25 centimes.[65]

Dawson acquired other specimens by exchange with institutions and individuals across Canada, the United States, and Europe. Cordial relations were soon restored with the Geological Survey of Canada. Three months after the survey moved to Ottawa, Dawson received shipments from it; within the next year, the Redpath Museum reciprocated by sending material to Ottawa. Dawson traded specimens regularly with curators at major museums abroad such as Henry Woodward, Keeper of the British Museum's Department of Geology. But it was especially to "surveys and private collectors in the United States" that Dawson looked.[66]

Earlier, Dawson had warned Thomas White, Member of Parliament, that the result of the Dominion government's transfer of the survey museum was "to annex us practically to the United States." Perhaps Dawson meant that he himself would look south for support. He eagerly swapped fossils with that country's foremost amateurs including Ralph Dupuy Lacoe; with state museum directors like James Hall in Albany, NY; and with the most distinguished local societies such as the Boston Society of Natural History, through the efforts of its officers Alpheus Hyatt and Samuel Scudder. He also arranged exchanges with curators in the largest museums in the land, for example with Richard Rathbun at the National Museum in Washington, DC, and R.P. Whitfield at the American Museum of Natural History in New York City. The Smithsonian Institution's Assistant Secretary, Spencer Baird, enticed Dawson to aid the institution's expedition to Ungava Bay by promising him the expedition's first series of duplicates — better than the specimens going to Ottawa — for the Redpath Museum.[67]

In Montreal, the brewer and banker J.H.R. Molson donated at least $500 and sometimes as much as $1,000 a year for the purchase of otherwise unobtainable collections. Molson's generosity enabled Dawson to buy rocks and fossils from naturalists and dealers overseas, including Anton Dohrn at the Zoological Station in Naples, the elderly Edward Charlesworth of London, Charles Moore in Liverpool, and August Krantz at Bonn. By the late 1880s the museum collections were valued at nearly $60,000.[68] Since funds for purchases were always limited, Dawson came to rely upon donations of specimens from friends in Montreal, elsewhere in Canada, and abroad, which were duly acknowledged in the annual reports of the museum and at quarterly intervals in the Montreal *Gazette*. Some of these acquisitions, such as Lieutenant Colonel Charles Coote Grant's collection of Silurian fossils, were invaluable additions to the museum's inventory. On the other hand, items like stuffed song sparrows and Baltimore orioles — accepted in order not to discourage or offend potential patrons — strained the museum's meager resources for display and preservation.

As George Brown Goode had pointed out, the uncritical acceptance of any gift might eventually radically alter the plan of a museum.[69] The Redpath Museum's annual report for 1896 urged the university to recognize the museum as "a permanent department of University expenditure" and to end its dependency upon "donations and private gifts." The report for 1898 noted that only $80, the interest on a special museum fund, was available for the purchase of specimens. In 1899 and again in 1900, the honorary curator, Bernard Harrington, communicated the museum's desperate financial plight to a meeting of the McGill University corporation and emphasized that there were no funds available whatsoever to increase its collections. He even argued somewhat facetiously that the lack of money to purchase specimens put the Redpath Museum in "a unique position among University Museums of the Continent."[70] The university nevertheless paid little attention to these complaints, and continued only to undertake general museum repairs and maintenance as it had been obliged to do from the outset. Unable to tie the growth of its collections to burgeoning national or even provincial pride, the Redpath Museum had no resources to tap to permit continued development and expansion.

BUENOS AIRES

Like their fellow directors on other continents, museum curators in Argentina acquired specimens through purchase, exchange, and donation. Operating under financial constraints as elsewhere, but employing unusually large staffs, Argentine museums turned the efforts of their permanent employees towards expanding their holdings. Periodically collectors, preparators, and travelling naturalists scoured the Argentine countryside, still rich in paleontological and ethnological treasures.

The Buenos Aires Museum, like the Canterbury Museum, exhibited arts and antiquities in addition to more scientific material. When Hermann Burmeister began to organize the natural history division during the early 1860s, he singled out as its most remarkable specimens the fossilized remains of the large extinct sloth-like mammals that had once roamed the Pampas. The museum possessed leg bones and other pieces of *Megatherium*, the most complete individual *Glyptodon* anywhere, at least three species of *Mylodon*, and the only known *Toxodon* skull. The Madrid Museum, the sole possessor of a superior specimen, got hold of an entire *Megatherium* skeleton before the Argentine government prohibited exportation of these rarities.

Ornithology was also strong, with 500 species (1,500 specimens) of European and South American birds, or about half the species native to the latter continent. The collections of amphibians and fish, even after the removal of some badly preserved specimens, were of less general interest. Scientific study in these departments required complete specimens kept in spirits, and for this Burmeister needed additional funds to import good glass containers from Europe. He did, however, classify the Argentine species, emphasizing the fish of the Rio de la Plata in particular. Winter humidity threatened the insect collection, leading Burmeister to bemoan the lack of separate quarters to dry out those specimens. Unfortunately the public were denied the sight of a beautiful collection of Brazilian and Argentine butterflies because light had destroyed their brilliant tropical colors. Burmeister also arranged 550 species of shells, gathered from all over the world, and added a local collection besides.

Apart from these zoological items, the Buenos Aires Museum's botanical collections included specimens of Paraguayan timber and a herbarium of European plants purchased in France. The mineralogical division included many items from Chilean mines, as well as a cabinet with more than 700 specimens from France which had been acquired during Carlos Ferrari's directorship in the 1820s. Although a small part of this section had been arranged to show different classes of metals and their relationships, the vast majority of items were neither numbered nor scientifically named.[71]

Constrained by the collections at hand, Burmeister nonetheless tried to fashion the Buenos Aires Museum into an institution more attractive to the Argentine public. He featured local materials arranged to exhibit the organization of natural kingdoms. His personal concerns lay in the areas of entomology and paleontology, and he encouraged Argentinians to give specimens and money to these departments.[72] At his own expense, he explored portions of the hinterland and donated the collections to the museum. He also traded duplicate specimens with naturalists in Europe and North America. He obtained, for example, 650 North American birds from the Smithsonian Institution, Malaysian specimens from the Genoa natural history museum, and European birds from the University of Griefswald.[73]

Except for a few cases of special acquisitions through individual or institutional good will, most additions to the collections of the Buenos Aires Museum came about in one of three ways. On occasion the government granted a special sum that permitted Burmeister to purchase materials that he deemed especially desirable. In one case, he asked to spend 2,000 pesos on a collection of fossil bones which contained many pieces missing from the museum's holdings.[74] Out of his regular budget, a second source of acquiring materials, Burmeister found the capital to buy a collection of Brazilian butterflies for 6,500 pesos and to place 1,000-peso orders with the natural history supplier Henri C. Deyrolle in Paris.[75] In 1872 alone, he spent more than 13,000 pesos on new objects.[76] With 90 percent of the museum's budget going to salaries, little was left over for purchases, and, as the third option, the museum had to depend on the activity of its permanent staff for new accessions.

From the beginning Burmeister employed a hunter (*cazador*) whose entire job was to search for new materials to be exchanged, sold, or added to the collections. From time to time the museum's preparator brought back objects from his travels. In addition, beginning in the early 1880s, a talented young Spaniard was hired as a collector (*colocado*) for the province of Buenos Aires. Any fossil bones he discovered which did not duplicate other museum specimens were to go to augment its holdings.[77] By 1885, Burmeister even suggested to the government that his budget for expanding the collections be reduced because of the activity of his regular staff in this area.[78] Collecting had virtually supplanted purchasing by this time, and Burmeister channelled uncommitted funds in other directions whenever possible.

A study of museum expenditures reveals that Burmeister was in fact more interested in developing the museum library — which won the praise of one foreign visitor — than the collections themselves. He favoured the library, he explained, because it was fundamental to any scientific work carried out on the collections. During the first six months of 1876 alone, Burmeister ordered books worth 18,000 pesos from bookstores in London and Paris. In 1882, a year when over 100 new works were added to the library, he spent 10,000 pesos on John Gould's five-volume work on hummingbirds.[79] Even in a typical year, Burmeister spent thousands of pesos on books from Germany, England, and France. These sums often amounted to more than ten times the annual expenditure on fossils or other additions to the collections. The emphasis on library accessions indicates that Burmeister gradually reoriented the Buenos Aires Museum to serve the needs of the serious scholar rather than to entertain and instruct the casual visitor. As a result, however, the museum was seen as neglecting its public function and became an easy target for government budget cutting.

LA PLATA

For Francisco Moreno, too, a proper library formed an essential part of the La Plata Museum. In order to provide adequate research materials for his hand-picked scientific staff, he donated and even catalogued his own 2,000-volume library. But he put special effort into expanding the museum collections. Called the "South American Livingstone" by one historian, Moreno's quasi-military collecting campaigns took him deep into Patagonia and other remote parts of the Argentine hinterland, notably dangerous and inhospitable country. There he discovered numerous ancient burial grounds and Indian camps. He collected 300 skulls of prehistoric man, and these whetted his appetite for the study of South American ethnology.[80]

When Moreno visited Europe in 1880, he set up exchanges with prestigious institutions and returned with objects to exhibit alongside comparable local Argentine materials. From the mid-1880s onward, Moreno was aided by the museum's travelling naturalists, among them Burmeister's son Carlos. Several Indians who had accompanied Moreno on his expeditions came to reside in the museum as living examples of their race. They posed for the artists who painted the splendid murals in the museum's rotunda, and one even acted as porter.[81]

Following in Hermann Burmeister's footsteps, Moreno put together the finest collection of Pampean mammal fossils in the world. These specimens, many of which were practically perfect, were displayed in the large interior halls of the main floor. Whale skeletons hanging from the ceiling of other galleries on the same floor won the praise of one visitor, Henry Holland, who rated them second only to the British Museum's collection, but better prepared. The first floor also exhibited vertebrate skeletons, mounted mammals and birds, and a mineralogical section. Extensive archaeological and ethnological collections were divided between the first and second floors.[82]

The La Plata collections benefited in particular from the hiring in 1886 of the paleontologist Florentino Ameghino as museum sub-director and secretary and of his brother Carlos, who served as travelling naturalist.[83] During the late 1880s, Moreno's principal concern became the expansion of his permanent staff of collectors, who searched the interior for specimens, although he also received materials by donation and through purchase. Quantity mattered to Moreno, who advocated displaying several examples of each species in order to demonstrate the different characteristics due to sex or age. By this time, the La Plata Museum boasted 100,000 specimens, including 1,000 skulls and 80 skeletons of prehistoric man.[84] Only strictly limited numbers of foreign specimens were displayed, and then solely for comparative purposes.

Moreno was driven to create a museum of international scientific renown, but the La Plata Museum's reputation rested exclusively on the completeness of its Argentine materials. The importance of its paleontological collections was shown to the scientific world when British Museum curator Richard Lydekker travelled there to study Argentine fossils during the early 1890s. He called them extraordinary and of worldwide interest.[85] Henry Ward was no less impressed; he placed the La Plata Museum (whose collections he appraised at $250,000) in the same category as those of Berlin and Vienna or Harvard's Museum of Comparative Zoology. The La Plata Museum was the only museum he had seen in South America where all was orderly and systematic. Furthermore, he knew of no other in the world with so many large, mounted, fossil skeletons.[86]

CONCLUSION

Apart from the problem of acquisition itself, the question of what to display and how to display it was answered in slightly different ways in each colonial situation. Both the Buenos Aires and Canterbury museums exhibited art and antiquities as well as natural history materials of every description. The National Museum of Victoria showed technological applications alongside the different departments of natural science. Although natural history remained the dominant concern of museum directors, they held different views of the proper balance between local and foreign specimens. The La Plata Museum, for example, included foreign objects only for purposes of comparison with local materials. The number of native objects, in fact, vastly outstripped those from abroad, since Moreno believed in exhibiting more than one example of each Argentine species or variety. On the other hand, the Canterbury Museum and the National Museum of Victoria emphasized general exhibits of foreign materials and segregated local materials into distinct geographical groupings.

In the greater significance that they attached to objects acquired abroad, both Australasian museums became heavily involved in international networks of purchase and exchange. South American museums increasingly relied upon collectors working in the hinterland whose finds enriched their holdings. By the early twentieth century, this method — using a museum's permanent staff — became the dominant method of expanding collections and eventually drove most natural history dealers out of business. Redpath Museum, unlike South American institutions, acquired local materials in a haphazard fashion, depending heavily on donations from the community.

The balance between serving the local populace and providing facilities for serious researchers also varied from place to place. Ostensibly, a museum could do both; the Canterbury Museum, for example, helped scholars by storing study collections away in drawers, but treated the general public to a series of interesting exhibits of local and foreign materials. By the closing decades of the nineteenth century, the National Museum of Victoria had both improved its research record and attained unprecedented attendance levels. These twin successes vindicated McCoy's aggressive acquisitions policy and offered solace for the attacks of politicians.

In all the cases examined here, colonial museum builders dealt with Europeans from a surprising position of strength. Far from being unwitting dupes, directors in the hinterland knew exactly which specimens they wanted to expand their collections, as well as the best ways of

Table 6
Size and Estimated Value of Collections

Museum	Date	Number of Specimens	Value
Canterbury	early 1870s	56,000	£10,000
Peter Redpath	late 1880s	n.a.	$60,000
La Plata	late 1880s	100,000	$250,000
National Museum of Victoria	late 1880s	500,000[1]	£50,000

n.a.: not available
[1]In 1900

Source: CPL, "Statement of Specimens in the Canterbury Museum," 30 Sept. 1873; F. Moreno, "Museo La Plata: Informe Preliminar," *Boletín del Museo La Plata* (1888): 4; R.T.M. Pescott, *Collections of a Century: the History of the First Hundred Years of the National Museum of Victoria* (Melbourne: National Museum of Victoria, 1954), 86.

obtaining them. Cooperative colleagues in London and elsewhere greatly eased their work, and less supportive men like Richard Owen could be sidestepped altogether. Colonial directors knew how to bargain with metropolitan museum curators and dealers, as the tone of Frederick McCoy's correspondence shows, for example. Once the power of his purse diminished, McCoy still managed to make the "merchant-naturalists" jump and to keep them dangling for payment for years. Haast, who favoured exchanges for building his collection, refused to sacrifice his materials for anything below their market value. Increasingly, he too turned to purchase as funds became available, for he had received too much unwanted material by exchange.[87] Indeed, the exchange system fell out of common usage as it began to be blamed for losing precious items to the colonies forever and for its failure to establish a *quid pro quo*.[88]

The result of all this activity was the creation of collections in overseas museums, which were remarkable for their quantity and quality. By the end of the century, most colonial museums had assembled hundreds of thousands of specimens valued at hundreds of thousands of dollars (see Table 6). Many of their holdings were, in fact, unique, and European curators had to travel to these distant places to see them. For museum builders like Burmeister, McCoy, and Dawson, such intellectual pilgrimages would have been reward enough for their labours.

CHAPTER FIVE

Conclusion

The degree of civilization to which any nation, city or province has attained is best shown by the character of its public museums and the liberality with which they are maintained.

George Brown Goode[1]

COLONIAL MUSEUMS
COME OF AGE

By around 1900, museums in the hinterland finally attained the kind of international stature of which their directors had dreamed. European naturalists travelled thousands of miles to view collections whose richness had become legendary. Paradoxically, reputations started to be based upon local materials, not on the extensive collections of foreign specimens that colonial curators had devoted so much attention to acquiring. Indeed, as the century drew to a close, many of the precepts that had guided these directors during most of their lives were increasingly challenged. Colonial museums, like those elsewhere, testified to defunct disciplinary imperatives. Certainly by the outbreak of the First World War, the "museum movement" had waned everywhere. In science, as in other realms, the old order of cathedrals and palaces gave way to unadorned functionalism that lacked any scale or grandeur.[2]

Just when museums were ceasing to be the principal loci of activity in the biological and earth sciences, a number of museums in the hinterland had joined the major leagues. Gradually they became less dependent upon metropolitan museums for materials, men, and models, and instead began to help and cooperate with each other. Communications improved, exchanges increased, and staff travelled from one museum to another for visits or new jobs.[3] Moving away from its former dependence on the whims of metropolitan museum curators and natural history dealers, the Canterbury Museum began to swap specimens with the South Australian Museum in Adelaide, which in turn traded with the Indian Museum in Calcutta and the Australian Museum in Sydney. One of the collectors at the National Museum of Victoria, Gerard Krefft, went on to become curator of the Australian Museum.[4] The tremendously popular international exhibitions, first held in the colonies in the 1870s and 1880s, were instrumental in stimulating these arrangements by increasing communication among colonial institutions.[5].

Skills and experience were thus transmitted from one museum in the hinterland to another. This process built up an invaluable reservoir of information. Colonial museums even began to collect statistics on museums in similar circumstances in order to buttress their arguments for increased support.[6] For example, Ronald Trimen, the director of the South African Museum in Cape Town, asked Julius Haast for information on the Canterbury Museum's constitution, funding, and staff, explaining that "our position is so extremely unsatisfactory in almost every way, that I am anxious to be possessed of trustworthy data respecting kindred Institutions in other colonies."[7] When F.W. Hutton at the Auckland Museum heard of Haast's grant of £14,000 in 1874, he wrote that the spur of competition would do him "all the good in the world" in getting funding in Auckland.[8].

At the same time that colonial museums began to look to each other for support, they started to view their own local resources with a new appreciation. Increasingly legislators forbade the exportation of rare natural history and ethnological materials.[9] Directors carefully reviewed exchange arrangements in order to ensure that only desirable materials were received and that they carried approximately the same value as those sent out. One historian of Australian museum development calls it an "ironic and unanticipated reversal" that the staff of "imperially-inspired museums" became so active in preserving local flora and fauna instead of sending them home to the mother country for examination and study.[10] This new spirit of cooperation and self-respect contributed to the independence and international reputation of colonial museums overseas.

Despite constant complaints of underfunding and the aggressive postures adopted by directors like Haast and McCoy, colonial museums fared well at the international level. The tens or even hundreds of thousands of dollars expended on new museum buildings were reasonable and respectable amounts by world standards. Average annual budgets of around $5,000 put them on a par with the better museums in Europe and the United States, apart from major national repositories. The Canterbury Museum, though near the bottom of our scale in terms of economic resources, still ranked tenth or eleventh in the world according to one newspaper account of the day.[11]

All the museums considered here nevertheless faced shrinking budgets after an initial burst of financial enthusiasm associated with their foundation or revitalization. In addition, funding depended upon the whims of government legislators or college trustees, making colonial museums especially vulnerable to changing political or economic fortunes. Because long-term financial commitments were especially problematic and staffing was the most expensive single budget item, colonial institutions clearly lagged behind the most important metropolitan museums in terms of number of personnel. But again, compared to state or provincial museums in Europe or North America, the museums considered here ranked with the best.

One measure of the popular success of colonial museums is their attendance figures, ranging from around 2,000 for the Redpath Museum to perhaps 50,000 for the Canterbury Museum. During the late 1880s, the National Museum of Victoria counted over 130,000 annual visitors. By 1900, the British Museum and the American Museum of Natural History each received around 400,000 annually; on the other hand, another major institution, Prague's Bohemian Museum, had an attendance of just 90,000 in one year.[12] Given the small size of the populations that these museums served, attendance figures in the colonies were respectable by world standards.

Another indicator both of the importance of museums in the hinterland and of how well they served researchers is the size of the collections that they brought together. By 1900, the Redpath Museum possessed nearly 80,000 specimens, and the National Museum of Victoria, where McCoy's acquisitions policy had been particularly aggressive, claimed over 500,000 objects. A few decades earlier the La Plata Museum had counted 100,000 specimens and the Canterbury Museum over half that number. With an average of hundreds of thousands of specimens, these museums made a reasonable showing against metropolitan museums. The world giant of the day was probably the National Museum in Washington, D.C., with more than three million items by the early 1890s.[13]

THE "MUSEUM MOVEMENT"
WANES AROUND 1900:
FINANCIAL RESTRAINT

These successes, however, were maintained with difficulty as other developments threatened the realization of the dreams of colonial museum builders. All the museums considered here experienced some economic setbacks within a few decades of their foundation. By 1900, the financial health of many of them had deteriorated further. For museums with relatively large budgets, such as the La Plata Museum or the National Museum of Victoria, restraint meant reducing salaries or firing a few staff. For the more poorly funded museums, however, no excess could be trimmed without cutting into the heart of the institution. At the Peter Redpath Museum, for example, the services of the anatomical preparator were not fully exploited since the museum could not afford to purchase jars to hold specimens.[14]

Part of the reason for this belt-tightening was the general economic depression that had gradually spread beyond the boundaries of Western Europe during the closing decades of the nineteenth century. But even at the best of times, the colonist who resisted "any demand which reduced his income," would oppose the taxation necessitated by the expansion of museums or indeed for the support of any kind of social and educational programmes.[15] As George Basalla has pointed out, colonial scientific institutions enjoyed an "easy success" due to their reliance on established European scientific traditions. Continued and sustained support was another matter altogether, especially as it required "the arduous task of ... fostering attitudes conducive to the rapid growth of science."[16]

During even relatively prosperous periods, it was easy for income not to match expenditures — as the National Museum of Victoria found because of McCoy's extravagance and the Redpath Museum discovered around 1900 — simply because of the nature of museum building. As soon as the museum began to buy specimens, costs rose rapidly. Curators required more staff members in order to care for, clean, and preserve these materials; as the collections grew, the workload of course increased, and this necessitated the hiring of additional personnel. Display or storage cases were another need. Very quickly cabinets outstripped the floor and wall space in the museum, thereby creating a need for major renovation or expansion of the building. A continuous preoccupation with obtaining more specimens, more workers, and more room meant that ambitious museum directors constantly clamored for more money.

POLITICAL SQUABBLES

Except during the first heady years of museum building, institutions in the hinterland chronically failed to get adequate and consistent funding. This state of affairs came about in part because decisions about financial matters were always made by authorities outside the museums themselves. Museums and their directors often found themselves helpless pawns in a larger political game, subject to the whims of legislators or trustees. The very creation of the Redpath and La Plata museums, as well as the decline of the Buenos Aires Museum, resulted from political accident. In these instances, the hegemony or location of the dominant museum in the area was upset abruptly as the result of a broader shift in government policy. Colonial museums were easily embroiled in complex strategies or confounded with issues of little relevance to their particular situations.

On the other hand, in their eagerness to obtain revenue, directors were willing accomplices for politicians and quick to jump on any available bandwagon. Haast, at a time when provincial (rather than federal) forces held sway in New Zealand, wrote to one local politician that the establishment of a museum in Christchurch would help to counteract centralizing tendencies.[17] He went on to advise one of his fellow curators in South Australia that "there is a wonderful power of persuasion in having MP's [sic] on your own ground and putting their august noses upon your specimens in the Museum ... Do likewise and the future of your Institution will be secured." The La Plata Museum became involved in schemes for national aggrandisement, since, as part of its founding rhetoric, it promised to advance geological, geographic, and cartographic studies that would allow a rational demarcation between Chile and Argentina.[18] Once political winds shifted, however, as they would in New Zealand, Argentina, and elsewhere, museums risked losing their *raison d'être* and thus their support.

The fact that by the late nineteenth century, a number of museums existed in every country treated here meant that the dynamics among institutions became very complicated indeed. Haast's confidant Hutton, then director of the museum at Otago University in Dunedin, explained that he had to exploit interprovincial rivalry in order to get anything done, though he felt not "a particle of jealousy" towards Haast. If the Canterbury Museum did not exist, claimed Hutton, there would be none in Dunedin either.[19] In other cases, however, jealousy was more real than apparent. McCoy, although unrivalled in Australia for his museum-building skills, urged one supplier to make haste in order "to insure our work being done before that of any other body." In Australia, he insisted, "time is of more value than anything else."[20] The institutions considered here were perhaps especially competitive because, as provincial museums for the most part, none was the sole national repository for the country in question. In addition, national institutions in other scientific realms — geological surveys, astronomical observatories, or government laboratories — always threatened to divert interest and resources away from museums.[21]

INDIVIDUAL EXERTION

A second reason for the poor financial health of museums in the hinterland was their intensely strong association with individuals and their particular aspirations. This came about in part because museum builders generally were the founders, predominant donors, and major developers of their institutions for nearly half a century. As long as directors like Haast and McCoy — whose aggressive attitudes towards their respective governments were remarkable — flourished, the institutions prospered. But when long-time patrons and directors declined, so did the museums. McCoy's death meant that ambitious opponents with different views about the place and functions of the National Museum of Victoria rushed in to fill the gap left by his absence. At the La Plata Museum, Moreno tendered his resignation when legislators decided to subordinate the museum to the local university. In the case of the Redpath Museum, no new supporters emerged to replace Dawson or the early curators and patrons whose enthusiasm and dedication had launched the museum. As a result, said one critic, the museum that had been among the top six in North America fell into a state of neglect by the early twentieth century. Sixty years after Haast's death, according to one biographer, "his museum, once hailed as the best south of the line, seemed but an overcrowded storehouse.[22]

The intense personalism, if one may call it that, of colonial museums sets them apart from dominant trends in the development of scientific institutions during the late nineteenth and early twentieth centuries. The onset of the era of "big science" meant typically that scientific activity began to involve teamwork, elaborate technology, and massive government expenditure. Even for museums in the twentieth century, complex bureaucracies employing a highly specialized, professional staff made the emergence of a dominant individual leader increasingly improbable.[23] The curators of colonial museums, in contrast, failed to become cooperative coworkers, due to the overwhelming preponderance of the director and the atomizing forces of understaffing. These tendencies undermined arguments for funding, and resources all too easily went instead to competing scientific bodies. Colonial natural history museums thus appear as a particular stage in the evolution of scientific institutions, but organizations better adapted to the demands of twentieth-century scientific activity would soon displace them from an important role.[24]

A NEW MISSION FOR COLONIAL MUSEUMS: LOCAL STUDIES AND THE UNIVERSITY

Responding to transient political pressures or being utterly dependent upon individual personalities was no substitute for a coherent plan or program of museum development. As George Brown Goode and other leading museum theorists had pointed out, a well-defined purpose or fixed point of reference was one of the cardinal needs of proper museum administration.[25]. Almost by default, colonial museums found a purpose by the end of the century, though one more restricted in scope than most early directors would have endorsed. It involved, first, a renewed interest in playing to one's strengths — that is, a decision to focus upon local materials. Second, museums to a greater extent than before cultivated liaisons with universities in the area.

From the beginning, some museums had been more interested than others in emphasizing native flora and fauna. The most committed to this principle had been the La Plata Museum, where foreign specimens were exhibited only insofar as they helped to illustrate or explain Argentine specimens. The least interested was the National Museum of Victoria, aggressively international in orientation due to the attitude of its director, McCoy. Somewhere between the two extremes fell the Redpath Museum, the Buenos Aires Museum, and the Canterbury Museum. The Redpath was slightly more inclined to present materials from the immediate neighbourhood than the rest of the world. Local specimens were, of course, less expensive and easier to procure than foreign objects. This decision to concentrate on local materials had, however, certain shortcomings; some critics felt that ethnological and miscellaneous "relics with no intrinsic value" made the Canterbury Museum seem too much like an "old-fashioned country museum."[26]

Around this time, even in Europe and the United States, curators began to express new interest in museums whose purviews were restricted to materials from the immediate environment. Anton Fritsch, director of the Bohemian Museum in Prague, argued that the primary function of a museum ought to be the exhibition of national flora and fauna (fossil and recent) and mineral resources and indigenous products. All foreign material, retained only for comparative purposes, ought to be kept in drawers and cabinets. Fritsch expressed little sympathy for the storehouse concept followed by many European museums, which held limited interest for the citizenry. Comprehensive world museums, he insisted, were not only undesirable but more and more impossible.

Goode concurred that national museums were necessarily less attractive than local museums because, given their vast holdings, materials had to be strictly classified and there was no room to introduce extraneous explanatory matter. Individual objects, though not general relationships, were better studied in small museums.[27] In England, curator Henry Howorth suggested that even the Natural History Museum ought to contain materials from the London area, since it functioned as a local natural history museum for the city. Provincial museums likewise should place greater stress on the locality, since people everywhere were most interested in "the things they can find about home and know something of," reasoned Howorth.[28]

Echoing these sentiments, colonial curators elsewhere looked to the Canterbury Museum — not even the most parochial in the group — as a particularly good example of a museum featuring indigenous materials. Ronald Trimen explained to Haast that "the only way in which a small local Museum can become of value or have any distinguishing character" was to emphasize local products. Only as space and means increased should other regions be included.[29] The South Australian Museum in Adelaide set out to acquire a reputation for Australian paleontology and ethnology, as the Canterbury Museum had in New Zealand.[30] The quest for comprehensiveness had meant all too often that foreign collections occupied too much space, yet remained inadequate for serious study.

Along with the desire to assemble exotic foreign collections, earlier dreams of popular education and mass appeal also changed by the end of the century. This attempt to entertain a wide audience and at the same time meet the requirements of a few researchers — the much-heralded new museum idea of several decades earlier — began to seem increasingly unworkable. Instead of serving as cathedrals of science for the general populace, museums were to be temples of scholarship for an elite group of scientists alone. "Education" began to refer to the specific needs of scholars rather than the rational entertainment of the public.[31] Yet even the decision exclusively to foster research created tension between the museum's function as an archive and its role in promoting scholarship.[32]

By the end of the century, museums found a more realistic role as organs of higher education, particularly through affiliation with local universities. Again, the museums considered here may be arranged on a spectrum, from the university-affiliated Peter Redpath Museum to the La Plata Museum, which had university status foisted upon it when it, along with the local university, was nationalized in 1906.[33] Both the Buenos Aires Museum and the National Museum of Victoria had always been closely associated with neighbouring universities, not only physically but administratively. While Burmeister had fought for autonomy for the Buenos Aires Museum, McCoy, in contrast, used the government museum for teaching purposes. In New Zealand, Julius Haast had always seen the Canterbury Museum as the starting point of higher education in the province and had urged the establishment of science lectures there. The museum finally "attracted" a university to the city with the foundation of the University of Canterbury in 1873.[34]

FINAL REFLECTIONS

In his pioneering survey of 1893, F.A. Bather distinguished colonial museums by their adaptation to local circumstances and their dependence upon foreign institutions. Certainly museums in the hinterland did follow metropolitan models and did import European staff. But the personnel often stayed on to shape a new kind of scientific career, while metropolitan patterns worked only insofar as local circumstances permitted. The very existence of these indigenous museums overseas, in fact, militated against extreme scientific dependence, because they protected local treasures against plunder by European institutions. They may be seen as encouraging the first steps toward scientific independence, in the sense that they provided a haven for natural resources and products of the locality. They came to offer, in addition, scientific training and a variety of positions to native talents inclined towards natural history.

Colonial museums flourished, however, only as long as the museum movement prospered elsewhere. As the youngsters who flocked to the Natural History Museum in South Kensington during the 1880s and 1890s grew to maturity, natural history museums began to lose their importance within the discipline of biology.[35] The natural sciences — now pursued by specialists in geology, zoology, botany and the like — moved towards the microscopic rather than the macroscopic. Even Darwinian evolution, which at first had accelerated the zeal to collect by rationalizing taxonomy and giving new scientific significance to varieties, seemed to offer more to the geneticist in the laboratory than to the ornithologist or mammalogist in the field. Those who remained in the field found that new techniques like photography provided better data about ecology and behaviour than a wealth of museum specimens.[36]

Developments outside the biological sciences, such as the rise of public and private research institutes and the remarkable expansion of universities, also diverted resources and interest away from museums to other scientific endeavours. Nevertheless, until the second or third decade of the twentieth century, natural history was largely caught up with the development of museums. To look at these museums today is to glimpse magnificent monuments to a remarkably hardy and adaptable tradition.

Notes

The following abbreviations are used in the notes.

AAAS   American Association for the Advancement of Science

BAM   Museo Argentino de Ciencias Naturales "Bernardino Rivadavia" archives: Correspondencia de oficio del Director del Museo Público de Buenos Aires

BM(NH)   British Museum (Natural History) archives, London

CAM   Manuscripts Reading Room, University of Cambridge Library. Correspondence of Adam Sedgwick, add. 7652, Cambridge

CAM(CD)   Manuscripts Reading Room, University of Cambridge Library. Correspondence of Charles Darwin, Cambridge

CM   Canterbury Museum, Christchurch

CPL   Canterbury Public Library, New Zealand Room, Christchurch

DSB   Dictionary of Scientific Biography

HAW   Henry A. Ward papers, University of Rochester Library, Special Collections, Rochester, NY

JWD   John William Dawson papers, McGill University Archives, Montreal

KEW   Correspondence of William Jackson Hooker, Royal Botanic Gardens archives, Kew, England

LPM   La Plata Museum, folder of documents on the museum, La Plata

MC   McGill University Archives, Montreal

MCZ   Museum of Comparative Zoology Archives, Harvard University, Cambridge, Mass.

ML   McCoy correspondence, Mitchell Library, Sydney

NMV   National Museum of Victoria, Melbourne

SI   Smithsonian Institution Archives, Washington, DC

TL   von Haast papers (MS 37), Turnbull Library, Wellington, NZ

CHAPTER ONE

1 David Murray, *Museums: Their History and Their Use*, 3 vols. (Glasgow: James MacLehose & Sons 1904), 1:224. An abstract of the present book has appeared as "Cathedrals of Science: The Development of Colonial Natural History Museums During the Late Nineteenth Century," *History of Science* 25 (1987): 279–300. An earlier version of this chapter also has been published as "Civilizing by Nature's Example: The Development of Colonial Museums of Natural History, 1850–1900," in N. Reingold and M. Rothenberg, eds., *Scientific Colonialism: a Cross-cultural Comparison* (Washington, DC: Smithsonian Institution Press 1987), 351–77.

2 Exceptions to this general rule are the interesting study by Camille Limoges, "The Development of the Muséum d'Histoire Naturelle of Paris, *c*. 1800–1914" in Robert Fox and George Weisz, eds., *The Organization of Science and Technology in France 1808–1914* (Paris: Maison des Sciences de l'Homme and Cambridge: Cambridge University Press 1980), 211–40; and the "Papers Presented at the International Conference on the History of Museums and Collections in Natural History," *Journal of the Society for the Bibliography of Natural History* 9 (1980): 365–670. S. Bedini traces the development of museums devoted to physical sciences and technology in "The Evolution of Science Museums," *Technology and Culture* 6 (1965): 1–29. See also the recent study by Sally Gregory Kohlstedt, "Australian Museums of Natural History: Public Priorities and Scientific Initiatives in the 19th Century," *Historical Records of Australian Science* 6 (1983): 1–29.

3 Murray, *Museums*, 1: 5–19, 186–208.

4 Carl von Linné (Linnaeus), *Reflections on the Study of Nature*, tr. James E. Smith (London: G. Nicol 1785), 24ff.

5 For example, see A.R. Wallace, "Museums for the People," *MacMillan's Magazine* 19 (1869): 244–50.

6 Suggested by Germain Bazin, *The Museum Age* (New York: Universe Books 1967), 8, and also by the director of the British Museum in the 1930s, Sir Frederic Kenyon; see Kenneth Hudson, *Museums of Influence* (Cambridge: Cambridge University Press 1987), 74.

7 For a discussion of these issues see Duncan F. Cameron, "The Museum: a Temple or a Forum" in the special issue of UNESCO's *Journal of World History* 14 (1972): 194, and Kenneth Hudson, *A Social History of Museums: What the Visitors Thought* (London: Macmillan & Co. 1975), 13, ch. 2.

8 Hudson, *Museums of Influence*, 83.

9 As a result of his study of museums for UNESCO, Hudson remarks that he was struck by the rapidity with which a Western European institution, the museum, has spread all over the world, and by the ways in which it has been adapted to different cultures. He admits that the mechanisms by which this process has occurred have been studied in only the most rudimentary way.

Hudson, *Museums of Influence*, 1–3.

10 J. Mordaunt Crook, *The British Museum* (London: Allen Lane 1972), 200, 204ff., 207. See Henry Scadding's description of the interior of the New Museum in his "On Museums and Other Classified Collections, Temporary or Permanent, as Instruments of Education in Natural Science," *Canadian Journal of Industry*, n.s. 13 (1871): 15–16. Superb illustrations and discussion of the architecture of the South Kensington Museum appear in Mark Girouard's *Alfred Waterhouse and the Natural History Museum* (London: British Museum 1981), 38, and elsewhere. See also Richard Owen, *The Life of Richard Owen*, 2 vols. (London: John Murray 1895), 2: 53; A.B. Meyer, *Studies of the Museums and Kindred Institutions of New York City, Albany, Buffalo, and Chicago, with Notes on Some European Institutions* (Washington, DC: Government Printing Office 1905), 523–4; A.E. Gunther, *A Century of Zoology at the British Museum Through the Lives of Two Keepers, 1815–1914* (London: Dawsons 1975), 349. William T. Stearn, *The Natural History Museum at South Kensington* (London: Heinemann 1981), 44–5, 49–52, describes the interior embellishments.

11 Meyer, *Studies of Museums*, 526. E.O. Hovey, "Notes on Some European Museums," *American Naturalist* 32 (1898): 708–10, 712; O.C. Farrington, "Notes on European Museums," *American Naturalist* 33 (1899): 775–6.

12 Hudson, *Museums of Influence*, 73.

13 Among the various suggestions for organizing natural history museums are those of Louis Agassiz, "On the Arrangement of Natural History Collections," *Annals and Magazine of Natural History*, 3d ser., 9 (1862): 415–19; W.A. Herdman, "An Ideal Natural History Museum," *Proceedings of the Literary and Philosophical Society of Liverpool* 12 (1887): 61–81; A.L. Herrera, "Les musées de l'avenir," *Memorias de la Sociedad Científica "Antonio Alzale"* 9 (1896): 221–51.

14 Meyer, *Studies of Museums*, 325, credits Louis Agassiz with being first to articulate this principle, which was later adopted in Europe.

15 William Henry Flower, *Essays on Museums and Other Subjects Connected with Natural History* (London: Macmillan & Co. 1898), 13, 15–19.

16 Ibid., 16–19, 38.

17 J.E. Gray, "Museums, Their Use and Improvement," *Report of the 34th Meeting of the British Association for the Advancement of Science; held at Bath* (London: John Murray 1865), 77–8. On Gray's view of museums, see also Stearn, *Natural History Museum*, 35–6.

18 Richard Owen, *On the Extent and Aims of a National Museum of Natural History* (London: Saunders, Otley & Co. 1862), 54, 14, 22–3, 27, 70–3, 63. See also Stearn, *Natural History Museum*, 36–7, 57.

19 Gunther, *Century of Zoology*, 349, 352.

20 David Van Keuren suggests that the museums of local history and anthropology established by Augustus Pitt-Rivers during the 1870s and

1880s offered an alternative to the new museum idea. See David Van Keuren, "Museums and Ideology: Augustus Pitt-Rivers, Anthropological Museums, and Social Change in Later Victorian Britain," *Victorian Studies* 28 (1984): 171–89. Indeed, Flower himself had insisted that only in national museums could research be as important as instruction; elsewhere, education should be the primary function; see Flower, *Essays*, 38.

21 A.C.L. Guenther, "Objects and Uses of Museums," *Report of the 50th Meeting of the British Association for the Advancement of Science; held at Swansea* (London: John Murray 1880), 591–2; Flower, *Essays*, 43–5; Farrington, "Notes," 764; Anton Fritsch, "The Natural History Departments of the Bohemian Museum," *Natural Science* 8 (1896): 168–71; Meyer, *Studies of Museums*, 584–5, 597. Jean Schopfer, "Natural History Museum at Paris," *Architectural Record* 10 (1900): 55–75.

22 Anton Fritsch, "The Museum Question in Europe and America," *Museums Journal* 3 (1904): 252; J.E. Gray, "Museums," 77.

23 A. Fritsch, "Museum Question," 170–1; Farrington, "Notes on Museums," 764.

24 Meyer, *Studies of Museums*, 324. For a survey of British museums at about this time, see Thomas Greenwood, *Museums and Art Galleries* (London: Simpkin, Marshall & Co. 1888).

25 L.V. Coleman, *The Museum in America*, 2 vols. (Washington, DC: American Association of Museums 1939), 2:13,14.

26 Meyer, *Studies of Museums*, 329; George Brown Goode, ed., *The Smithsonian Institution, 1846–1896. The History of Its First Half Century* (Washington, DC: DeVinne Press 1897), 328–30.

27 The success of the habitat idea depended upon the remarkable advances in taxidermy realized at Ward's Natural Science Establishment. Ward's students — including W.T. Hornaday, F.S. Webster, and F.A. Lucas — took up posts at the National and American museums and at lesser US institutions as well. See G.B. Goode, "Recent Advances in Museum Method," *Report of the U.S. National Museum for the Year Ending 30 June 1893* (Washington, DC: Government Printing Office 1895), 42–5.

28 G.B. Goode, "The Principles of Museum Administration," in Museums Association, *Report of Proceedings ... 1895 ... in Newcastle* (London: Museums Association 1895), 69–148.

29 Edward P. Alexander points out that more than fifty years later, Goode's *Principles* were reprinted and distributed for the use of museums in South Africa. See E.P. Alexander, *Museum Masters: Their Museums and Their Influence* (Nashville: American Association for State and Local History 1983), 296.

30 Suggested by A.E. Gunther, who also introduces the category of colonial museums; see Gunther, *Century of Zoology*, 152–3, 320–2, and his *Founders of Science at the British Museum, 1753–1900* (Suffolk: Halesworth Press 1980), 125.

31 F.A. Bather, "Some Colonial Museums," Museums Association, *Report of Proceedings ... 1894 ... in Dublin* (London: Museums Association 1895), 231–3.

32 Ibid., 235.

33 Wallace, "Museums for the People," 245; John Ellor Taylor, ed., *Notes on Collecting and Preserving Natural History Objects* (London: Hardwicke & Bogue 1876), 2; Scadding, "On Museums," 23; Guenther, "Objects and Uses," 593.

34 Hudson, *Social History*, 24.

35 George Basalla, "The Spread of Western Science," *Science* 156 (1967): 611–22.

36 Roy MacLeod, "On Visiting the 'Moving Metropolis': Reflections on the Architecture of Imperial Science," *Historical Records of Australian Science* 5 (1982): 1–16.

37 Ibid., 9–11.

38 Michael Worboys, "The British Association and Empire: Science and Social Imperialism," in Roy MacLeod and Peter Collins, eds., *The Parliament of Science: The British Association for the Advancement of Science, 1831–1981* (Northwood, Middlesex: Science Reviews Ltd. 1981), 170–87.

39 Ian Inkster, "Scientific Enterprise and the Colonial 'Model': Observations on the Australian Experience in Historical Context," *Social Studies of Science* 15 (1985): 677–704.

40 Daniel R. Headrick, *The Tools of Empire: Technology and European Imperialism in the Nineteenth Century* (New York and Oxford: Oxford University Press 1981).

41 Lucile H. Brockway, *Science and Colonial Expansion: The Role of the British Royal Botanic Gardens* (New York: Academic Press 1979).

42 Lewis Pyenson, *Cultural Imperialism and Exact Sciences: German Expansion Overseas, 1900–1930* (New York: Peter Lang 1985).

43 Raymond Grew, "The Case for Comparing Histories," *American Historical Review* 85 (1980): 773–4.

44 Donald Fleming, "Science in Australia, Canada, and the United States: Some Comparative Remarks," *Actes du Dixième Congrès International d'Histoire des Sciences* (Paris: Hermann 1962), 179–96, esp. 179–81, 183. Another explicitly comparative study is Lewis Pyenson's "Incomplete Transmission of a European Image: Physics at Greater Buenos Aires and Montreal, 1890–1920," *Proceedings of the American Philosophical Society* 122 (1978): 91–114.

45 Fleming, "Science in Australia," 182.

46 Editors of a volume on colonial cities make an argument for juxtaposition rather than comparison. See Robert J. Ross, Gerard J. Telkamp et al., eds., *Colonial Cities: Essays on Urbanism in a Colonial Context* (Dordrecht: Martinus Nijhoff 1985), 6.

47 H.A. Miers and S.F. Markham, *A Report on the Museums and Art Galleries of*

British Africa (Edinburgh: T. & A. Constable 1932), viii, 3, 10, 17, 31–2.

48 S.F. Markham and H. Hargreaves, *The Museums of India* (London: Museums Association 1936), 3, 21, 49, 57–8.

49 Henry Marc Ami, *Report on the State of the Principal Museums in Canada and Newfoundland* (London: British Association for the Advancement of Science 1897). Even in 1937, educational institutions in Quebec housed 116 museum collections, 100 of which were devoted to natural sciences, while the other 8 provinces could claim only 64 similar collections among them. See also Archie F. Key, *Beyond Four Walls: The Origins and Development of Canadian Museums* (Toronto: McClelland & Stewart 1973), 110. For a history of the Royal Ontario Museum, see Lovat Dickson, *The Museum Makers: The Story of the Royal Ontario Museum* (Toronto: Royal Ontario Museum 1986).

50 Henry A. Miers and S.F. Markham, *A Report on the Museums of Canada* (Edinburgh: T. & A. Constable Ltd. 1932), 8–9, 27.

51 L.V. Coleman, *Directory of Museums in South America* (Washington, DC: American Association of Museums 1929), 3–4, 8.

52 S.F. Markham and W.R.B. Oliver, *A Report on the Museums and Art Galleries of New Zealand* (London: Museums Association 1933), 75–81; S.F. Markham and H.C. Richards, *A Report on the Museums and Art Galleries of Australia* (London: Museums Association 1933), 2–6, 27–8. For Australian museums see also Kohlstedt, "Australian Museums."

53 R.T.M. Pescott, *Collections of a Century: The History of the First Hundred Years of the National Museum of Victoria* (Melbourne: National Museum of Victoria 1954), 37; Bather, "Colonial Museums," 226–9; "The Difficulties of the Australian Museum," *Natural Science* 15 (1899): 318.

54 HAW, J.W. Dawson to H.A. Ward, 25 Jan. 1881.

55 ML, William Denison to Frederick McCoy, 29 June [1859?].

56 Markham and Richards, *Museums of Australia*, 29; Gerard Krefft, "The Improvements Effected in Modern Museums in Europe and Australia," *Transactions of the Royal Society of New South Wales* (1868): 20; Ronald Strahan, *Rare and Curious Specimens; An Illustrated History of the Australian Museum, 1827–1979* (Sydney: Australian Museum 1979), 31; Herbert M. Hale, "The First Hundred Years of the Museum: 1856–1956," *Records of the South Australian Museum* 12 (1956): 73.

57 Warwick Armstrong, "Land, Class, Colonialism: The Origins of Dominion Capitalism," in W.E. Willmot, ed., *New Zealand and the World: Essays in Honour of Wolfgang Rosenberg* (Christchurch: University of Canterbury), 28–44, esp. 28.

58 H.S. Ferns, *Britain and Argentina in the Nineteenth Century* (Oxford: Oxford University Press 1960), 487. D.C.M. Platt takes issue with an earlier articulation of this view, presented by John Gallagher and Ronald Robinson in "The Imperialism of Free Trade," *Economic History Review* 6 (1953–4): 1–15,

as well as with Ferns's definitive work. See D.C.M. Platt, "Imperialism of Free Trade: Some Reservations," *Economic History Review* 21 (1968): 296–306, and his *Finance, Trade and Politics in British Foreign Policy, 1815–1914* (Oxford: Oxford University Press 1968), 308–68. In his "Further Objections to an Imperialism of Free Trade," *Economic History Review* 26 (1973): 77–91, however, Platt reluctantly approves the use of the term "informal empire" to describe Britain's relationship with Argentina after the 1860s.

59   Gallagher and Robinson, "Imperialism," 15.

60   Ferns, *Britain and Argentina*, 487.

61   D.C.M. Platt, "Canada and Argentina: The First Preference of the British Investor, 1904–14," *Journal of Imperial and Commonwealth History* 13 (1985): 77–92, esp. 78. In *The Prairies and the Pampas: Agrarian Policy in Canada and Argentina, 1880–1930* (Stanford, CA: Stanford University Press 1987), 9, Carl E. Solberg suggests that demographic and economic trends serve to bring Argentina and Canada together, yet demarcate them from their continental neighbours.

62   Armstrong, "Land, Class, Colonialism," 31.

63   Gallagher and Robinson, "Imperialism," 9–10.

64   Barrie Dyster, "Argentine and Australian Development Compared," *Past and Present* 84 (1979): 91–110, esp. 91; Warwick Armstrong and John Bradbury, "Industrialisation and Class Structure in Australia, Canada and Argentina: 1870 to 1980," in E.L. Wheelwright and K. Buckley, eds., *Political Economy of Australia* (Sydney: ANZ Book Co. 1983), 5:43–74. See also E.L. Wheelwright, "Australia and Argentina: A Comparative Study," in his *Radical Political Economy* (Sydney: ANZ Book Co. 1974), 270–96, esp. 270–1.

65   A recent comparative study of science funding suggests that the extraordinarily high level of British support for museums during this period reveals a "passion for museums" in that country. See Nathan Reingold and Joel N. Bodansky, "The Sciences, 1850–1900: A North Atlantic Perspective," *Biological Bulletin* 168 (1985): 48.

66   A.F.W. Plumptre, "The Nature of Political and Economic Development in the British Dominions," *Canadian Journal of Economics and Political Science* 3 (1937): on 506.

67   H.H. Howorth, "Some Casual Thoughts on Museums," *Natural Science* 7 (1895): 98.

68   Bather, "Colonial Museums," 207; CPL, Haast to Edward Jollie, 6 Sept. 1870, 7.

69   William Swainson, *Taxidermy, Bibliography, and Biography* (London: Longman, Orme, Brown, Green & Longmans 1840), 77–8.

70   Markham and Richards, *Museums of Australia*, 23. According to Coleman, the Buenos Aires Museum possessed around 90 percent of all known species of Tertiary mollusca. See Coleman, *Museums in South America*, 26.

CHAPTER TWO

1   SI, F. Moreno to G.B. Goode, 31 Aug. 1896.

2   As J.B. Morrell has claimed for chemistry laboratories in "The Chemist Breeders: The Research Schools of Liebig and Thomas Thomson," *Ambix* 19 (1972): 1–46. Kenneth Hudson attributes the extraordinarily influential role of the Natural History Museum to the special personal attributes of its director, in this case W.H. Flower. See Kenneth Hudson, *Museums of Influence* (Cambridge: Cambridge University Press 1987), 73.

3   Edward P. Alexander, *Museum Masters: Their Museums and Their Influence* (Nashville: American Association for State and Local History 1983), 15–16, 297. Alexander quotes from William Henry Flower, *Essays on Museums and Other Subjects Connected with Natural History* (London and New York: Macmillan & Co. 1898), 12, and from George Brown Goode, "A Memorial of George Brown Goode, Together with a Selection of His Papers on Museums and on the History of Science in America," in SI, *Annual Report for 1897*, part 2; *Report of the U.S. National Museum* (Washington, DC: Government Printing Office 1901), 202.

4   Ann Moyal also uses the term "museum builder" to describe Frederick McCoy's work in Australia. See A. Moyal, *"A Bright and Savage Land": Scientists in Colonial Australia* (Sydney: Collins 1986), 94–5. Lovat Dickson uses "museum makers" to describe the founders of the Royal Ontario Museum; see his *The Museum Makers: The Story of the Royal Ontario Museum* (Toronto: Royal Ontario Museum 1986).

5   See ch. 3, p. 53, on the Philosophical Institute of Victoria and its museum.

6   G.C. Fendley, "Sir Frederick McCoy," *Australian Dictionary of Biography* 5:134–6; "Johann Franz Julius von Haast," *DSB* 5:610–12. For additional discussion of Haast, especially of his geological work, see David Oldroyd, "Haast's Geological Theories and the Opinions of his European Contemporaries," *Journal of the Royal Society of New Zealand* 3 (1973): 5–14, and Haast's obituary in the *Quarterly Journal of the Geological Society* (1888): 45–7.

7   Geoffrey Blainey, *A Centenary History of the University of Melbourne* (Melbourne: Melbourne University Press 1957), 11; NMV, miscellaneous correspondence, 1854/1931, Salter to McCoy, 6 July [1867].

8   Carlos Berg, "Notice nécrologique sur le docteur Hermann Burmeister," *Annales de la Société Entomologique de France* 63 (1894): 705–12; "Haast," *DSB*.

9   Blainey, *Centenary History*, 37; Ernest William White, *Cameos from the Silverland; Or the Experiences of a Young Naturalist in the Argentine Republic*, 2 vols. (London: Van Voorst 1881–2), 1:198; Peggy Burton, *The New Zealand Geological Survey, 1865–1965* (Wellington: New Zealand Department of Scientific and Industrial Research 1965), 10–11.

10 Donald Fleming, "Science in Australia, Canada, and the United States; Some Comparative Remarks," *Actes du Dixième Congrès International d'His-*

toire des Sciences (Paris: Hermann 1962), 180.

11 Fendley, "McCoy."

12 George Basalla, "The Spread of Western Science," *Science* 156 (1967): 617.

13 Berg, "Notice"; E.O. Essig, *A History of Entomology* (New York: Macmillan & Co. 1931), 562–3; Aquiles D. Ygobone, *Francisco P. Moreno: Arquetipo de Argentinidad* (Buenos Aires: Orientacion Cultural Editores 1953), 245.

14 H.F. von Haast, *The Life and Times of Sir Julius von Haast* (Wellington: Avery Press 1948), 566. Recent scholarship corroborates Hooker's comment. See Robert A. Stafford, "Geological Surveys, Mineral Discoveries, and British Expansion, 1835–71," *Journal of Imperial and Commonwealth History* 12 (1984): 5–32, esp. 20, who shows that extensive colonial service began to constitute a drain on British geology, and on the survey in particular, as early as the mid-1860s.

15 "John William Dawson," *DSB* 3:607–9; "Haast," *DSB*; see also D.R. Oldroyd, "Nineteenth Century Controversies Concerning the Mesozoic/Tertiary Boundary in New Zealand," *Annals of Science* 29 (1972): 39–57; Fendley, "McCoy"; Sally Gregory Kohlstedt, "Australian Museums of Natural History: Public Priorities and Scientific Initiatives in the 19th Century," *Historical Records of Australian Science* 6 (1983): 1–29, 60*n*; Ygobone, *Moreno*, 248.

16 CAM, II.HH.63, McCoy to Sedgwick, 15 July 1872; Blainey, *Centenary History*, 39. Kohlstedt, "Australian Museums," 4–5, notes the importance of the Geological Survey for Australian museums. See also Fendley, "McCoy"; David Wilson, *Rutherford: Simple Genius* (London: Macmillan & Co. 1983), 21.

17 Fendley, "McCoy."

18 CAM (CD), Darwin to Hooker, 25 May 1870.

19 CAM (CD), Darwin to Hooker, 4 Nov. 1862.

20 CAM (CD), Hooker to Darwin, 2 Nov. 1862.

21 JWD, Henry S. Williams to J.W. Dawson, 6 Jan. 1881.

22 Marcelo Montserrat, "La Mentalidad Evolucionista: una Ideologia del Progreso," in Gustavo Ferrari and Ezequiel Gallo, eds., *La Argentina del ochenta al centenario* (Buenos Aires: Editorial Sudamericana 1980), 788.

23 ML, CY 499, J.S. Henslow to G.B. Airy, 26 May 1854, 713; Ann Mozley Moyal, *Scientists in Nineteenth Century Australia: A Documentary History* (Melbourne: Cassell Australia 1976), 425–6.

24 Fendley, "McCoy."

25 Moyal, *Bright and Savage Land*, 146–7.

26 Although McCoy always remained opposed to these topics. See Geoffrey Serle, *The Golden Age: A History of the Colony of Victoria, 1851–1861* (Melbourne: Melbourne University Press, 1963), 366; Kohlstedt, "Australian Museums"; Fendley, "McCoy".

27 Blainey, *Centenary History*, 38.

28 Florentino Ameghino, *Obras Completas y correspondencia científica de Floren-tino Ameghino*, ed. Alfredo J. Torcelli, 24 vols. (La Plata: Taller de impre-siones oficiales 1935), 21 : 415–16; H. Burmeister, "Observations on the Vari-ous Species of *Glyptodon* in the Public Museum of Buenos Aires," *Annals and Magazine of Natural History*, 3d ser. 14 (1864): 81.

29 The controversy, in which Haast maintained that the moa was extinct before the Maoris arrived, mostly appears in the *Transactions of the New Zealand Institute*, although Quatrefages responds to Haast in the *Annales des sciences naturelles* (Nov. 1883). See T. Lindsay Buick, *The Mystery of the Moa: New Zealand's Avian Giant* (New Plymouth, NZ: T. Avery & Sons 1931), esp. 332, 131*n*; Moyal, *Scientists in Australia*, 131–2; Moyal, *Bright and Savage Land*, 120–3. See also T.G. Vallance, "The Fuss About Coal: Troubled Relations Between Palaeobotany and Geology" in D.F. Carr and S.G.M. Carr, eds., *Plants and Man in Australia* (Sydney: Academic Press 1981), 136–76, esp. 148ff; Elena Grainger, *The Remarkable Reverend Clarke* (Melbourne: Oxford University Press 1982), 220–5. Stafford, "Geological Surveys," 10, also discusses the acrimonious disputes that developed between colonial geologists over the stratigraphic classifications of coal deposits.

30 McCoy challenged Agassiz as well. See P. de Malpas Grey Egerton, "Obser-vations on Mr. McCoy's Paper on Some Fossil Fish of the Carboniferous Period," *Annals of Natural History* 2 (1848): 189–90, and McCoy's reply, 277–80. Just before he left for Australia, McCoy had a dispute with the eminent French naturalist Henri Milne-Edwards, who accused McCoy of plagiarism. See A. Sedgwick, "A Reply to Two Statements Published by the Paleontographical Society, in Their Volume for 1852, One ... Reflecting on Professor McCoy," *Annals and Magazine of Natural History* 2d ser. 13 (1854): 280–92; H. Milne-Edwards, "A Reply to Professor Sedgwick's Article ...," *Annals and Magazine of Natural History* 2d ser. 13 (1854); 469–72.

31 Moreno and Burmeister argued about the origins of the Tertiary fauna of Patagonia; see Ygobone, *Moreno*, 250; Ameghino, *Obras Completas*, 21 : 423, 411, 459.

32 Ameghino, *Obras Completas*, 20 : 447–8; Ygobone, *Moreno*, 376–8, 381–2; Fernando Marquez Miranda, *Ameghino: una Vida Heroica* (Buenos Aires: Editorial Nova 1951), 311.

33 ML, CY 499.

34 Ibid., A. Sedgwick to McCoy, n.d. [1855?]; J.W. Clark and T.M. Hughes, *The Life and Letters of the Reverend Adam Sedgwick*, 2 vols. (Cambridge: Cambridge University Press 1890), 2 : 194*n*.

35 ML, CY 499, Sedgwick to McCoy, n.d. [1855?].

36 CAM, McCoy to Sedgwick, 15 July 1872 (II.HH.63).

37 ML, CY 499, R.I. Murchison to McCoy, 12 May 1859; Edward Forbes to McCoy, 12 Nov. 1855 [sic.]; CAM, II.HH.63, McCoy to Sedgwick, 15 July 1872.

38 JWD, J.W. Dawson to William Williamson, 11 Sept. 1871. The Royal Society published only an abstract of Dawson's lecture "On Pre-Carboniferous Floras of North-eastern America," *Proceedings of the Royal Society of London* 18 (1869–70), 333–5. See Frederick Burkhardt, Sydney Smith, et al., eds., *A Calendar of the Correspondence of Charles Darwin, 1821–1882* (New York/London: Garland Publishing 1985), letter 7198.

39 See CAM (CD), Hooker to Darwin, 2 Nov. 1862; Darwin to Hooker, 12 Nov., 4 Nov., 24 Dec. 1862. Hooker was referring to his *Outlines of the Distribution of Arctic Plants*.

40 CAM (CD), Hooker to Darwin, 22 May 1870.

41 · For example, CAM (CD), Darwin to Hooker, 4 Nov. 1862, and elsewhere.

42 CAM (CD), Hooker to Darwin, 22 May 1870; Darwin to Hooker, 12 Nov. 1862.

43 It is especially interesting that Dawson's basic objection to Darwin's *Origin of Species* was that its conclusions were not supported by sufficient evidence. For a thoughtful discussion of Dawson's review of the *Origin* in the *Canadian Naturalist* see A.B. McKillop, *A Disciplined Intelligence: Critical Inquiry and Canadian Thought in the Victorian Era* (Montreal: McGill-Queen's University Press 1979), 99ff.

44 CAM (CD), Hooker to Darwin, 22 May 1870. Richard Yeo suggests that statements about method function as "argumentative devices" in scientific controversies, with each opponent accusing the other of infringing "orthodox" procedure; R. Yeo, "An Idol of the Market-place: Baconianism in Nineteenth Century Britain," *History of Science* 23 (1985): 283.

45 CAM (CD), Hooker to Darwin, 22 May 1870.

46 CAM, II.G.14a, McCoy to Sedgwick, 14 Dec. 1857; II.G.14b, 15 April 1858; II.CC.1, 24 May 1856.

47 ML, CY 499, Sedgwick to McCoy, 5 Oct. 1872.

48 British Library, add. mss. 44027, Samuel Butler papers, fol. 122, Butler to Haast, 14 Nov. 1865; von Haast, *Life of Haast*, 778.

49 Von Haast, *Life of Haast*, 775–6, 453.

50 Ernest Scott, *A History of the University of Melbourne* (Melbourne: Melbourne University Press 1936), 35.

51 McCoy's biographer, for example, speaks of a lack of professional employment that discouraged students from pursuing scientific training at this time; Fendley, "McCoy." See also B.A. Houssay, "La Personalidad de German Burmeister," *Physis* 29 (1942): 281.

52 As Burmeister complained publicly in the *Anales*. According to his biographer, as sole scientific officer McCoy found his energies and curiosity totally absorbed in classifying the museum's flood of acquisitions; see Fendley, "McCoy."

53 G.B. Goode, "The Principles of Museum Administration," Museums Association, *Report of Proceedings ... 1895 ... in Newcastle* (London: Museums

Association 1895), 78, 86.

54 On McCoy's reluctance to hire other scientific officers, see Kohlstedt, "Australian Museums," 167n.

55 As Moreno claimed to have done at the La Plata Museum. See Francisco Moreno, "Museo La Plata: Informe Preliminar," *Boletin del Museo La Plata* (1888): 4.

56 See ch. 4 for a discussion of these enterprises.

57 BAM, 26 Nov. 1866.

58 Ameghino, *Obras Completas*, 21:599–600.

59 R.T.M. Pescott, *Collections of a Century: the History of the First Hundred Years of the National Museum of Victoria* (Melbourne: National Museum of Victoria 1954), 42; NMV, letterbook 1, 381, McCoy to Gerrard, 24 Aug. 1861.

60 Roswell Ward, *H.A. Ward: Museum Builder to America* (Rochester: Rochester Historical Society Publications 1948) 24:172, 211; Sally Gregory Kohlstedt, "Henry A. Ward: The Merchant Naturalist and American Museum Development," *Journal of the Society for the Bibliography of Natural History* 9 (1980): 647–61, esp. 658, 30n.

61 HAW, T.F. Cheeseman to H.A. Ward, 29 April 1885.

62 See Andreas Reischek, *Yesterdays in Maoriland; New Zealand in the Eighties* (London: J. Cape 1930). This is a translation of his *Sterbende welt, zwölf jahre forsherleben aus Neuseeland*. On Haast's relationship with Reischek see von Haast, *Life of Haast*, 796–801, esp. 799–800.

63 Pescott, *Collections*, 41. The same pattern prevailed in other colonial museums. A fireman, F.J. Rau, became a collector for the South Australian Museum in Adelaide. See Herbert M. Hale, "The First Hundred Years of the Museum, 1856–1956," *Records of the South Australian Museum* 12 (1956): 66–7.

64 Von Haast, *Life of Haast*, 797.

65 At the South Australian Museum, too, mobility was the rule in the 1880s: a collector became staff entomologist; the "labourer," head attendant; an assistant taxidermist, taxidermist and articulator; and the conservator, assistant director. See Hale, "First Hundred Years," 40.

66 Pescott, *Collections*, 77.

67 JWD, acc. 1602, 1b, minute book (1882-92), 74, 82, 113; acc. 1459, 1, minute book (1892-1917), 28–30, 36–7.

68 *Report of the Peter Redpath Museum for the Year 1897*, 24; JWD, acc. 1602, 1b, minute book (1882–92) 29.

69 At a salary of $1,000 a year, paid by McGill; see JWD, acc. 1459, 1, minute book (1892–1917) 55, 59.

70 HAW, J.W. Dawson to Ward and Howell, 9 April 1885; Dawson to Ward, 1 May 1885; acc. 1602, 1b, minute book (1882–92) 30, 51, 66, 115.

71 JWD, acc. 1602, 1b, minute book (1882–92), 81, 92, 103–4.

72 JWD, acc. 1459, 1, minute book (1892–17), 29, 36, 67.

73 "Summario sobre la fundacion y los progresos del Museo Público de Buenos Aires," *Anales del Museo Público de Buenos Aires* 1 (1864): 10.

74 BAM, Ministro de Gobierno de la Provincia to Burmeister, 4 May 1881, fol. 556.

75 Ameghino, *Obras Completas*, 21:213, 623.

76 "Proemio," *Anales del Museo* 2 (1870–4): iv.

77 BAM, 23 April 1867.

78 BAM, 7 Oct. and 27 Oct. 1868.

79 BAM, Burmeister to Ministro de Gobierno, 22 Sept. 1873, fol. 406.

80 BAM, Burmeister to Ministro de Gobierno, 4 April 1876.

81 BAM, Burmeister to Carlos D'Amico, 22 Jan. 1883, fol. 656; Burmeister to Juan Dillon, 3 Feb. 1883, fol. 707a.

82 For example, BAM, Burmeister to Faustino Jorge, 14 Feb. 1884, fol. 720.

83 BAM, Burmeister to Ministro de Instrucción Pública, 8 Jan. 1885, fol. 790.

84 BAM, Burmeister to Jorge.

85 BAM, Burmeister to Juan Dillon, 3 Feb. 1883, fol. 707a.

86 BAM, Burmeister to Juan Balestra, 4 Jan. 1892; Burmeister to Filemon Posse, 1 March 1890.

87 For a short biography of Berg, see Max Biraben, "Ciento Cincuenta Años de Zoologia Argentina," *Physis* 22 (1961): 10–11.

88 For Burmeister's critical view of Argentine scientists, see Ameghino, *Obras Completas*, 21:411.

CHAPTER THREE

1 Quoted in Archie F. Key, *Beyond Four Walls: The Origins and Development of Canadian Museums* (Toronto: McClelland & Stewart Ltd. 1973), 52. An earlier version of this chapter has appeared as "Henry Augustus Ward and Museum Development in the Hinterland, 1860–1890," *University of Rochester Library Bulletin* 38 (1985): 38–59.

2 George Brown Goode, "The Principles of Museum Administration," in Museums Association, *Report of Proceedings ... 1895 ... in Newcastle* (London: Museums Association 1895), 88–9.

3 Nikolaus Pevsner, *A History of Building Types* (London: Thames & Hudson 1976), devotes a section (ch. 8) to the architecture of nineteenth-century museums.

4 Gordon Biddle, *Victorian Stations: Railway Stations in England and Wales, 1820–1923* (Newton Abbot: David & Charles 1973), 119.

5 Banister Fletcher, *A History of Architecture on the Comparative Method*, 17th ed. (London: Athlone Press 1961), 1057, 1126.

6 "Museum Architecture," *Encyclopedia Britannica*, Chicago ed. (1970), 15:1033.

7 Jeffrey Richards and John M. Mackenzie, *The Railway Station: A Social His-*

tory (Oxford: Oxford University Press 1986), 23–4.

8 See Sophie Forgan, "Context, Image, and Function: A Preliminary Enquiry Into the Architecture of Scientific Societies," *British Journal for the History of Science* 19 (1986): 89–113. She discusses the social symbolism of various nineteenth-century architectural conventions (see 91 and elsewhere).

9 Mark Girouard, *Alfred Waterhouse and the Natural History Museum* (London: British Museum 1981), 25–6.

10 James Fergusson, *History of the Modern Styles of Architecture*, 3d ed., 2 vols. (London: John Murray 1891), 2:170.

11 Forgan, "Context," 112.

12 For the best appraisal of Ward and the significance of his enterprise, see Sally Gregory Kohlstedt, "Henry A. Ward: The Merchant Naturalist and American Museum Development," *Journal of the Society for the Bibliography of Natural History* 9 (1980): 647–61. See also Roswell Ward, *H.A. Ward: Museum Builder to America* (Rochester: Rochester Historical Society Publications 1948), 178–9, 185.

13 HAW, Edward Gerrard to H.A. Ward, 8 April 1881; Ward, *H.A. Ward*, 216–17.

14 H.F. von Haast, *The Life and Times of Sir Julius von Haast* (Wellington: Avery Press 1948), 787.

15 Joan P. Morrison, *The Evolution of a City: The Story of the Growth of Cities and Suburbs of Christchurch, the Capital of Canterbury, 1850–1903* (Christchurch: Whitcombe & Tombs 1948), 7; David Wilson, *Rutherford: Simple Genius* (London: Macmillan & Co. 1983), 13; W.J. Gardner, ed., *A History of Canterbury*, 2 vols. (Christchurch: Whitcombe & Tombs 1971), 2:235–8.

16 Alexander Middleton, *Hand Book of Information for Emigrants to New Zealand, Australia, Canada, the United States, British Columbia, and the Red River Settlements* (Glasgow: William Love & James Nimmo 1870), 13.

17 Henry Francis Wigram, *The Story of Christchurch* (Christchurch: Lyttelton Times 1916), 167; Gardner, *History*, 231, 239. For more information on the history of Canterbury province, see Samuel Butler, *A First Year in Canterbury Settlement* (Auckland: Blackwood & Janet Paul 1964) (first published in 1863). A history of the province was produced under the auspices of the Canterbury Centennial Historical and Literary Committee; see James Hight and C.R. Straubel, eds., *A History of Canterbury* (Christchurch: Whitcombe & Tombs 1957–65). See also (and especially) A.H. Reed, *The Story of Canterbury: Last Wakefield Settlement* (Wellington: A.H. & A.W. Reed 1949).

18 Arthur Gordon Butchers, *Centennial History of Education in Canterbury* (Christchurch: Centennial Committee of the Canterbury Education Board n.d. [1953]), 21.

19 A short historical sketch of the Philosophical Institute appears in P.B. Maling, *The Philosophical Institute of Canterbury: A Survey of the First Hundred Years* (Christchurch: Royal Society of New Zealand, Canterbury Branch

1962). See also Morrison, *Evolution of a City*, 151–2; Wigram, *Story of Christ-church*, 246; 171–3; Butchers, *Centennial History*, 200–2.

20 Wigram, *Story of Christchurch*, 163–4.

21 Gardner, *History of Canterbury*, 245, 293, 483–4; James Hight, *A Short History of the Canterbury College* (Auckland: Whitcombe & Tombs 1927), 121.

22 Richards and Mackenzie, *Railway Station*, 87.

23 Von Haast, *Life of Haast*, 601–2.

24 Ibid., 609, 623.

25 CPL, Canterbury Museum Records, Haast to W. Kennaway, 7 May 1872; von Haast, *Life of Haast*, 628.

26 Von Haast, *Life of Haast*, 630.

27 CPL, Canterbury Museum Records, Haast to W. Kennaway, 3 May 1872.

28 CM, Session 38, *Annual Report of the Canterbury Museum for the Financial Year Ending September 30, 1872*, Appendix A.

29 Hight and Straubel, *History of Canterbury*, 21.

30 Gardner, *History of Canterbury*, 336.

31 CM, Canterbury Provincial Secretary for Public Works, incoming letters, no. 220, Haast to Edward Jollie, 22 Feb. 1869; *Guide to the Collections in the Canterbury Museum*, 3d ed. (Christchurch: T.E. Fraser 1906), 1.

32 Von Haast, *Life of Haast*, 759, 764.

33 Ibid., 763–4, 805, 819, 822.

34 Ibid., 884–5, 887, 893.

35 Geoffrey Serle, *The Golden Age: A History of the Colony of Victoria, 1851–1861* (Melbourne: Melbourne University Press 1963), 369.

36 James Grant and Geoffrey Searle, eds., *The Melbourne Scene, 1803–1956* (Melbourne: Melbourne University Press 1957), 74–5, 77, 136; Maturin Murray Ballou, *Under the Southern Cross* (Boston: Ticknor & Co. 1888), 181, 189. See also A. Middleton, *Hand Book for Emigrants*, 37–9.

37 Ward, *H.A. Ward*, 214.

38 Thwing, who surveys the history of higher education in Australia and New Zealand, suggests that a "noble place" was given to education in Australasian civilization. See Charles Franklin Thwing, *Human Australasia: Studies of Society and of Education in Australia and New Zealand* (New York: Macmillan & Co. 1923), 115.

39 Wilfred Henry Newnham, *Melbourne: The Biography of a City* (Melbourne: F.W. Cheshire 1956), 178; Grant and Serle, *Melbourne Scene*, 40.

40 Alan Lindsey McLeod, ed., *The Pattern of Australian Culture* (Ithaca: Cornell University Press 1963), 173; Grant and Serle, *Melbourne Scene* 77–8; R.T.M. Pescott, "The Royal Society of Victoria from Then, 1854 to Now, 1959," *Royal Society of Victoria Proceedings*, n.s. 73 (1961): 1–40, esp. 2; Ballou, *Under the Cross*, 181.

41 S.F. Markham and H.C. Richards, *A Report on the Museums and Art Galleries of Australia* (London: Museums Association 1933), 5; Serle, *Golden Age*, 353;

R.T.M. Pescott, *Collections of a Century: The History of the First Hundred Years of the National Museum of Victoria* (Melbourne: National Museum of Victoria 1954), 4.

42 Newnham, *Melbourne*, 182. In 1855, the Philosophical Society of Victoria (founded 1854) and the Victoria Institute for the Advancement of Science (founded 1854) united to form the Philosophical Institute of Victoria; in 1859, this became the Royal Society of Victoria. In 1887, the Society absorbed the Microscopical Society of Victoria. See Pescott, *Collections*, esp. p. 2.

43 G.C. Fendley, "Sir Frederick McCoy," *Australian Dictionary of Biography* 5:134.

44 NMV, letterbook 1, McCoy to J.E. Gray, 24 Oct. 1860.

45 Pescott, *Collections*, 173 ff.

46 NMV, letterbook 2, "Return of the National Museum for 1861," 34.

47 Grant and Serle, *Melbourne Scene*, 78.

48 Pescott, *Collections*, 46–7, 51–4.

49 Ibid., 68.

50 Annual reports appear in the yearly *Report of the Trustees of the Public Library, Museums, and National Gallery of Victoria.*

51 Sally Gregory Kohlstedt, "Australian Museums of Natural History: Public Priorities and Scientific Initiatives in the 19th Century," *Historical Records of Australian Science* 6 (1983): 1–29; *Report of the Trustees ... for 1888, 1889, 1890.*

52 *Report of the Trustees ... for 1891.*

53 *Report of the Trustees ... for 1897.*

54 *Report of the Trustees ... for 1898.*

55 *Natural History of Victoria. Prodromus of the Zoology of Victoria; or, Figures and Descriptions of the Living Species of All Classes of the Victorian Indigenous Animals,* 2 vols. (Melbourne: J. Ferres 1885–90); *Prodromus of the Palaeontology of Victoria; or, Figures and Descriptions of Victorian Organic Remains* (Melbourne: G. Skinner 1874–82); Pescott, *Collections*, 43.

56 Pescott, *Collections*, 173.

57 *Ward's Natural Science Bulletin,* 1 Jan. 1882, 1; 1 July 1882, 2; HAW, J.W. Dawson to Ward and Howell, 26 Nov. 1880; Dawson to H.A. Ward, 9 Dec. 1880.

58 Leslie Roberts, *Montreal: From Mission Colony to World City* (Toronto: Macmillan & Co. 1969), 215, 202; Kathleen Jenkins, *Montreal: Island City of the St.Lawrence* (Garden City, NY: Doubleday & Co. 1966), 360–2, 374, 385.

59 Ibid., 369; John Irwin Cooper, *Montreal: A Brief History* (Montreal: McGill-Queen's University Press 1969), 59–60; AAAS, *Handbook for the City of Montreal and Its Environs, Prepared for the Meeting ... by a Member of the Local Committee* (Montreal: Gazette Printing Office 1882), 116.

60 The earliest letter located is dated 10 June 1869. See HAW, J.W. Dawson to H.A. Ward, 10 June 1869.

61 William Dawson, *Fifty Years of Work in Canada: Scientific and Educational* (London and Edinburgh: Ballantyne, Hanson & Co. 1901), 169–72.

62 "Notice of the Natural History Collections of the McGill University," *Canadian Naturalist and Geologist* 7 (1862): 221–3.

63 AAAS, *Handbook*, 89; JWD, acc. 927, no. 47, ref. 38, J.W. Dawson to Charles Tupper, 12 Feb. 1881; Public Archives of Canada, J.A. Macdonald Papers, vol. 313, J.W. Dawson to Thomas Ryan, 17 March 1881; JWD, acc. 927, no. 47, ref. 1b, "The Geological Survey," *The Gazette*(?) (Montreal).

64 Dawson, *Fifty Years*, 174; "The American Association: Opening the Redpath Museum," *Witness*, 25 August 1882; "The Peter Redpath Museum: Formal Opening of the Building," clipping dated 25 August 1882 in JWD, box 37; Stanley B. Frost, *McGill University for the Advancement of Learning*, 2 vols. (Montreal: McGill-Queen's University Press 1980), 2:243; J.W. Dawson, *In Memoriam: Peter Redpath, Governor and Benefactor of McGill University* (Montreal: "Witness" Printing House 1894), 17. For more information on the creation of the Peter Redpath Museum see Susan Sheets-Pyenson, "'Stones and Bones and Skeletons': the Origins and Development of the Peter Redpath Museum," *McGill Journal of Education* 17 (1982): 45–64, esp. 51–2.

65 *Guide to Visitors to the Redpath Museum of McGill University* (Montreal: 1885), 2; MCZ, J.W. Dawson to Alexander Agassiz, 18 July 1882.

66 By the early 1890s, evening entertainments were banned from the museum for fear that fire might result from the use of gas for illumination; see JWD, acc. 1459, 1, minute book (1892–1917), 10, 107; MC, corporation minutes (1889–94), 392.

67 But when the museum reduced the admission fee to 10¢, it claimed that the charge was "not imposed for revenue." See JWD, acc. 1602, 1b, minute book (1882–92), 128.

68 *Report of the Peter Redpath Museum for the Year 1886*, 82; *Report of the Peter Redpath Museum for the Year 1888*, 105; *Report of the Peter Redpath Museum for the Year 1890*, 127.

69 Ward, *H.A. Ward*, 233; HAW, notebook (1889), 41.

70 HAW, notebook (1889), 103; M.M. Ballou, *Equatorial America* (Boston and New York: Houghton, Mifflin 1892), 268–70; Guillermo Rawson, *Vital Statistics of the City of Buenos Aires* (New York: Appleton 1876), 3–4, 22–3; W.J. Holland, *To the River Plate and Back* (New York and London: Knickerbocker Press 1913), 161–2.

71 HAW, notebook (1889), 123–5.

72 L.V. Coleman, *Directory of Museums in South America* (Washington, DC: American Association of Museums 1929), 5; Angel J. Carranza, "Anales del Museo Público de Buenos Aires," *Revista de Buenos Aires* 8 (1865): 273–83, 442–6, 612–7, esp. 274; "Sumario sobre la fundación y los progresos del Museo Público de Buenos Aires," *Anales del Museo Público de Buenos Aires* 1 (1864): 1–11, esp. 3; J.J. Parodiz, *Darwin in the New World* (Leiden: Brill 1981), 71.

naturales," unpub. ms. in possession of the late José Babini, 5, 8–10; *Anales del Museo*, 1 (1864): 2–4; Eduardo L. Holmberg, "El Museo de Buenos Aires," *El Naturalista Argentino* 1 (1878): 33–43, esp. 36, 38.

74 Juan Carlos Zuretti, *Historia de la cultura argentina: Arte, ciencia*, 12th ed. (Buenos Aires: Itinerarium 1952), 185–6, 197.

75 The nucleus of the faculty, hired by Burmeister, included the botanist Paul Lorentz, the mineralogist Alfredo Stelner, Guillermo Bodenbender, and Oscar Doering.

76 Zuretti, *Historia*, 190–3; Julio R. Castiñeiras, *Historia de la Universidad de La Plata*, 2 vols. (La Plata: Universidad Nacional de La Plata 1938–40), 1:121.

77 The Parana museum was revived between 1884 and 1899 under the Italian Pedro Scalabrini. After another period of decline, it was re-created as a provincial museum in 1917. See Zuretti, *Historia*, 187–8.

78 F. Ameghino, "Informe sobre el Museo Antropológico y Paleontológico de la Universidad Nacional de Córdoba, durante el año 1885," *Boletín de la Academia Nacional de Ciencias, Córdoba* 8 (1885): 347–60.

79 Zuretti, *Historia*, 214.

80 José M. Gallardo, *El Museo de Ciencias Naturales en la Manzana de las Luces* (Buenos Aires: Imprenta Coni SACIFI 1976), 6; Antonio Lascano González, *El Museo de Ciencias Naturales de Buenos Aires: Su Historia* (Buenos Aires: Ediciones Culturales Argentinas 1980), 86; Max Biraben, *German Burmeister: su vida, su obra* (Buenos Aires: Ediciones Culturales Argentinas 1968), 30; *Anales del Museo* 1 (1864): 4; H. Burmeister, "Observations on the Various Species of *Glyptodon* in the Public Museum of Buenos Aires," *Annals and Magazine of Natural History*, 3d ser. 14 (1864): 81–97, esp. 81.

81 Information on the budget of the Buenos Aires museum comes from its archives. See especially BAM, file M, no. 486, 10 July 1876, Burmeister to Ministerio de Gobierno; ibid., no. 490, 10 Jan. 1877, "Gastos para el Museo en el año de 1876"; ibid., no. 505, 6 Jan. 1878, "Cuenta de gastos del Museo Público durante el año 1877."

82 "Proemio," *Anales del Museo* 1 (1864): iii–iv, esp. iii; Gallardo, *Museo de Ciencias*, 6.

83 Holmberg, "Museo de Buenos Aires," 33–8, 41.

84 Ibid., 38–9, 41–2.

85 BAM, file M, no. 556, 7 May 1881, Burmeister to Ministerio de Gobierno.

86 For example, see BAM, file M for 1884.

87 MCZ, H.A. Ward to Alexander Agassiz, 26 July 1889.

88 Gallardo, *Museo de Ciencias*, 9.

89 Ballou, *Equatorial America*, 247, 268; Thomas A. Turner, *Argentina and the Argentines, 1885–1890* (London: S. Sonnenschein 1892), 164–8; Holland, *River Plate*, 109–10. See also Emile Daireaux, *La vie et les moeurs à la Plata* (Paris: Hachette 1888), 398.

90 Holland, *River Plate*, 113; Daireaux *La Plata*, 395; HAW, notebook (1889),

125–6, 133, 138, 146.

91 Gallardo, *Museo de Ciencias*, 8–9; José Liebermann, "Francisco P. Moreno, Precursor Argentino," *Anales de la Sociedad Científica Argentina* 140 (1945): 396–427, esp. 417.

92 Universidad Nacional de la Plata, *Obra del Centenario del Museo de La Plata* (La Plata: Facultad de Ciencias Naturales y Museo 1977), 1 (*Reseña Histórica*): 6, 12.

93 Ibid., 8–9.

94 Ibid., 9–10.

95 Casteñeiras, *Historia*, 121.

96 Luis María Torres, ed., *Guía para Visitar el Museo de la Plata* (La Plata: República Argentina 1927), 3–5, 9.

97 SI, Moreno to G.B. Goode, 28 Dec. 1895.

98 Richards and Mackenzie, *Railway Station*, 62.

99 Holland, *River Plate*, 114–15, 119; *Obra del Centenario*, 13–15, 25–7; Torres, *Guía*, 7–8, 17.

100 Torres, *Guía*, 7; *La Prensa* (Buenos Aires), 16 Sept. 1934.

101 F. Moreno, "Breve Reseña de los progresos del Museo La Plata, durante el segundo semestre de 1888," *Boletín del Museo La Plata* (1889): 5–44, esp. 11–12, 18, 43.

102 F. Moreno, "Museo La Plata: Informe Preliminar," *Boletín del Museo La Plata* (1888): 3–35, esp. 12.

103 G.B. Goode, ed., *The Smithsonian Institution, 1846–1896. The History of Its First Half Century* (Washington, DC: De Vinne Press 1897), 328–30.

104 A.B. Meyer, *Studies of the Museums and Kindred Institutions of New York City, Albany, Buffalo, and Chicago, With Notes on Some European Institutions* (Washington, DC: Government Printing Office 1905), 526, 590; H. Bolton, "Provincial Museums and the Museums Association," Museums Association, *Report of Proceedings ... 1898 ... in Sheffield* (London: Museums Association 1899), 91.

CHAPTER FOUR

1 G.B. Goode, "The Principles of Museum Administration," in Museums Association, *Report of Proceedings ... 1895 ... in Newcastle* (London: Museums Association 1895), 78.

2 Gerard Krefft, curator of the Australian Museum in Sydney, claimed that J.E. Gray's views had been realized in Australia. See G. Krefft, "The Improvements Effected in Modern Museums in Europe and Australia," *Transactions of the Royal Society of New South Wales* (1868): 15–25, esp. 21.

3 As proposed by J.S. Henslow, one of McCoy's mentors, in "On a Typical Series of Objects in Natural History Best Adapted to Local Museums," *Report of the 25th Meeting of the British Association for the Advancement of Sci-*

ence; held at Glasgow (London: John Murray 1855), 111.

4 F.A. Bather, "Some Colonial Museums," Museums Association, *Report of Proceedings ... 1894 ... in Dublin* (London: Museums Association 1895), 199.

5 Goode, "Principles," 85.

6 Haast, for example, persuaded shipping companies to carry specimens for the Canterbury Museum free of charge. See H.F. von Haast, *The Life and Times of Sir Julius von Haast* (Wellington: Avery Press 1948), 803.

7 SI, Moreno to Goode, 28 Dec. 1895; Burmeister to Spencer Baird, 5 July 1871.

8 E.W. Swanton, "Some South African Museums," *Museums Journal* 1 (1901–2): 325–6; NMV, McCoy correspondence, box B, British Museum, 1854–1931, file 1857–90, Gray to McCoy, 20 Oct. 1858.

9 See J.M. Chalmers–Hunt, comp., *Natural History Auctions 1700–1972: A Register of Sales in the British Isles* (London: Sotheby Parke Bernet 1976); D.E. Allen, *The Naturalist in Britain: A Social History* (London: Allen Lane 1976), 35, 37, 80, 145–52; W.H. Brock, "The Development of Commercial Science Journals in Victorian Britain," in A.J. Meadows, ed., *Development of Science Publishing in Europe* (Amsterdam: Elsevier Science Publishers 1980), 101–2. Damon writes that, since a cheap parcel post has been established, he and Haast can exchange specimens without waiting for special opportunities; see TL, folder 50, Damon to Haast, 30 Jan. 1873. See also Howard Robinson, *The British Post Office: A History* (Princeton, NJ: Princeton University Press 1984), 394.

10 Chalmers-Hunt, *Natural History Auctions*, 35; Allen, *Naturalist*, 189. These descriptions are taken from advertisements that appeared in *Scientific Opinion* (1869–70), the *Scientific Record* (1864), the *Naturalist* (1857), and *Scientific Summary* (1870). These were all periodicals published in London. For full titles and more information see Susan Sheets-Pyenson, "Popular Science Periodicals in Paris and London: The Emergence of a Low Scientific Culture, 1820–1875," *Annals of Science* 42 (1985): 549–72.

11 Allen, *Naturalist*, 186; Chalmers–Hunt, *Natural History Auctions*, 15–16, 44–5.

12 *Scientific Opinion* (1869); *Scientific Record* (1864).

13 R.T.M. Pescott, *Collections of a Century: The History of the First Hundred Years of the National Museum of Victoria* (Melbourne: National Museum of Victoria 1954), 28.

14 Ronald Strahan, *Rare and Curious Specimens: An Illustrated History of the Australian Museum, 1827–1979* (Sydney: Australian Museum 1979), 15; Frederick McCoy, *On the Formation of Museums in Victoria* (Melbourne: Goodhugh & Hough 1857), 4, 12.

15 William T. Stearn, *The Natural History Museum at South Kensington* (London: Heinemann 1981), 57.

16 F.A. Bather, "Some Colonial Museums," in Museums Association, *Report*

of Proceedings ... 1894 ... in Dublin (London: Museums Association 1895), 221–5.

17 CAM, II.G.14b, McCoy to Sedgwick, 15 April 1858; II.CC.1, 24 May 1856. Henslow himself helped McCoy to procure a series of botanical models and specimens. See KEW, McCoy to Hooker, 25 Oct. 1861; ML, CY 499, Henslow to McCoy, 10 March 1859.

18 NMV, miscellaneous correspondence, 1854–1931, Salter to McCoy, 24 Oct. 186[?], 14 March 1862. Reeks declined McCoy's offer to pay him a commission of 5 percent as compensation for his trouble. See NMV, letterbook 2, McCoy to Reeks, 24 May 1862, 25 Jan. 1864.

19 NMV, letterbook 1, McCoy to Gray, 14 Sept. 1857, 24 Oct. 1860. Gray seems to have expected no recompense for his innumerable labours on McCoy's behalf. He told McCoy that he was happy to help because two of his nephews lived near Melbourne. See NMV, McCoy correspondence, box B, Gray to McCoy, 10 Dec. 1857. Gray perhaps felt obligated to McCoy because McCoy had earlier unsuccessfully petitioned Gray for the vacant paleontology keepership at the British Museum. See ML, CY 499, Gray to McCoy, 11 Sept. 1857 (1851?).

20 NMV, McCoy correspondence, box B, Gray to McCoy, 10 Dec. 1857, 14 Jan. 1858.

21 Chalmers-Hunt, *Natural History Auctions*, 102; NMV, letterbook 2, McCoy to Gray, 168, no. 63/18; ibid., 169, no. 63/104.

22 NMV, McCoy correspondence, box B, Gray to McCoy, 17 Sept. 1862, 25 March 1863, 10 April 1863, 29 Dec. 1866, 23 Dec. 1862; A.E. Gunther, *A Century of Zoology at the British Museum Through the Lives of Two Keepers, 1815–1914* (London: Dawsons 1975), 269.

23 NMV, letterbook 2, 40–1, McCoy to Francis Walker, 21 Feb. 1862; BM (NH), Owen correspondence, vol. 9, Hugh Cuming to Owen, 5 Nov. 1839, 1 Nov. 1837; Chalmers-Hunt, *Natural History Auctions*, 47.

24 NMV, letterbook 2, 155, McCoy to Cuming, 23 Dec. 1862; ibid., 111, no. 62/142; ibid., 338, 25 July 1864; ibid., 418, 22 Feb. 1865.

25 NMV, letterbook 4, 334; McCoy to Geale, 2 Sept. 1878; box of lists and correspondence with Geale, etc., Geale to McCoy, 16 May 1870, 9 May 1871, 22 June 1878.

26 NMV, Reeve box, Reeve to McCoy, 19 May 1862, 17 April 1862, 25 Aug. 1862, 17 April 1862, 22 Sept. 1862, 17 March 1863.

27 Ibid., 25 Aug. 1862, 22 Sept. 1862, 19 Nov. 1862, 19 May 1862, 18 Oct. 1862, 19 June 1864, 14 May 1866 (from Reeve's widow); NMV, invoice book, 239. According to Chalmers-Hunt (*Natural History Auctions*, 102), Stevens auctioned the Reeve shells, including the Metcalfe collection, at the end of May 1864.

28 NMV, letterbook 1, 339, McCoy to Damon, 25 April 1861; ibid., 394, 26 Sept. 1861; letterbook 2, 479, 25 March 1862; ibid., 336, 23 July 1864; ibid.,

336, 25 Nov. 1864; invoice book, 179–84; Damon box, Damon to McCoy, 24 June 1862, 29 Dec. 1875.

29 Edward Gerrard, Sr. (1811–1910) was hired by the Department of Zoology at the British Museum in 1841 and he served as an attendant until 1896. Together with his son Edward, he founded a taxidermy firm in 1850, which operated from Camden Town somewhat later. See Gunther, *Century of Zoology*, 268–9, 115*n*, 276*n*; Stearn, *Natural History Museum*, 167; Sue Herriott, ed., *British Taxidermists: A Historical Directory* (Leicester: Leicester Museums 1968); R.W. Ingle, "A Century of Zoological Curating: Past and Present Aspects," information sheet for Centenary Open Days, British Museum (Natural History), Dept. of Zoology; *Proceedings of The Linnean Society of London* 123 (1911): 37–9, obituary of Edward Gerrard, Sr. Special thanks to D.E. Allen for information on this point.

30 TL, folder 66, Edward Gerrard to Haast, 3 July 1879, 3 March 1882.

31 Du Chaillu fell afoul of the simmering feud between Owen and Gray. See Gunther, *Century of Zoology*, 132–4, and his *Founders of Science at the British Museum, 1753–1900* (Suffolk: Halesworth Press 1980), 123–4. See also the *Athenaeum* for May and June 1861.

32 NMV, letterbook 2, 328, McCoy to Gerrard, 24 June 1864; ibid., 268, 25 Jan. 1864. For the cost of Du Chaillu's collections, see E.G. Allingham, *A Romance of the Rostrum* (London: H.F. & G. Witherby 1924), 61–2.

33 NMV, letterbook 1, 289, McCoy to Gerrard, 24 Oct. 1860; ibid., 381, 24 Aug. 1861; ibid., letterbook 2, 268, 25 Jan. 1864; ibid., McCoy to Gould, 25 Oct. 1862.

34 HAW, McCoy to Ward, 7 April 1885.

35 HAW, J.W. Dawson to H.A. Ward, 9 Aug. 1882; "Eighty Natural Science Cabinets ... ," *Ward's Natural Science Bulletin*, 1 July 1882, 2. In this circular, Ward lists 80 purchasers of natural history cabinets valued at $1,000 or more; McGill ranks 49th.

36 Pescott, *Collections*, 62. See, for example, the *Report of the Trustees of the Public Library, Museums, and National Gallery of Victoria* for 1881.

37 Pescott, *Collections*, 51, 69–73.

38 Ibid., 77–8.

39 *Report of Trustees* for 1895, 1897, 1898.

40 Pescott, *Collections*, 86.

41 CM, session 26, no. 57, "Canterbury Museum: Notes on the Collections belonging to the Province of Canterbury," 19–34. S.H. Jenkinson, *New Zealanders and Science* (Wellington: Department of Internal Affairs 1940), 41.

42 CM, Canterbury Provincial Secretary for Public Works, inwards letters, no. 220, Haast to Jollie, 22 Feb. 1869. For example, see CM, session 32, no. 17, "Progress Report by the Director of the Canterbury Museum, 1 Jan. to 30 Sept. 1869," 5–8; session 35, no. 43, "Report on the Canterbury Museum ... for the year ending 30 Sept. 1871," 18–19; von Haast, *Life of Haast*, 606.

These sources give the following tallies:

Category	New Zealand	Foreign
Mammals	7	44
Birds	18	93
Geology and Paleontology	4,617	7,134

43 CPL, Haast to Jollie, 6 Sept. 1870, 6–7.

44 Von Haast, *Life of Haast*, 603.

45 CPL, Haast to Jollie, 6 Sept. 1870, 2–3.

46 M.M. Ballou, *Under the Southern Cross* (Boston: Ticknor & Co. 1888), 317; TL, Darwin to Haast, 28 Jan. 1868; A.H. Reed, *The Story of Canterbury: Last Wakefield Settlement* (Wellington: A.H. & A.W. Reed 1949), 238; Jenkinson, *New Zealanders*, 42; BM (NH): Owen correspondence, vol. 14, Haast to Owen, 5 April 1868; TL, folder 26, A. Agassiz to Haast, 26 Nov. 1868.

47 TL, folder 283, newspaper clipping. See also W.R.B. Oliver, *The Moas of New Zealand and Australia*, Dominion Museum Bulletin no. 15 (Wellington: Dominion Museum 1949), 6.

48 Von Haast, *Life of Haast*, 3, 781.

49 TL, folder 125, Owen to Haast, 26 May 1867.

50 A moa skeleton (not a composite of two or more species) brought 48 guineas around 1900. See Allingham, *Romance*, 168.

51 BM (NH), Owen correspondence, vol. 14, Haast to Owen, 10 Jan. 1872, 29 Sept. 1873.

52 Von Haast, *Life of Haast*, 453; TL, folder 125, Owen to Haast, 16 Dec. 1873; BM (NH), Owen correspondence, vol. 9, Haast to Owen, 14 March 1874.

53 Agassiz offered Haast casts instead of specimens; see TL, A. Agassiz to Haast, 26 June 1866; folder 68, Günther to Haast, 7 May 1874.

54 BM (NH), Owen correspondence, vol. 14, Haast to Owen, 5 April 1868. The discovery of moa bones at Glenmark, near Christchurch, in 1866 and 1867 initiated this process. See TL, folder 63, Flower to Haast, 15 Nov. 1871.

55 This object could apparently be obtained only in England. Once in New Zealand, the glass case holding the head was kept covered out of consideration for Maori sensitivities. See von Haast, *Life of Haast*, 632–3.

56 TL, folder 63, Flower to Haast, 15 May 1869, 18 July 1874, 30 Sept. 1872, 10 Dec. 1875, 20 Oct. 1873.

57 TL, folder 50, Damon to Haast, 23 Dec. 1870, 9 Jan. 1873, 27 Oct. 1874, 26 June 1877.

58 TL, folder 66, Gerrard to Haast, 24 Jan. 1879, 10 Aug. 1880. According to other accounts, too, Australian objects had lost their fascination by the early 1880s. See for example HAW, Gerrard to Ward, 14 Feb. 1883, 17 May 1885.

59 Von Haast, *Life of Haast*, 779–80.

60 Ibid., 625. CM, Session 41, "Letter from Dr. Haast ... with statement of specimens," 8 June 1874.

61 CM, session 35, 15.

62 Von Haast, *Life of Haast*, 606, 609; CPL, "Statement of specimens in the Canterbury Museum," 30 Sept. 1873.

63 William Dawson, *Fifty Years of Work in Canada: Scientific and Educational* (London and Edinburgh: Ballantyne, Hanson & Co. 1901), 176.

64 JWD, Peter Redpath to Dawson, 17 Jan. 1881.

65 JWD, George Mercer Dawson to Dawson, 20 June, 26 June, 17 July, 23 July, 24 Sept. 1882; Dawson to James Ferrier, 3 April 1884.

66 JWD, Robert Hamilton to Dawson, 12 Aug. 1881; A.H. Foord to Dawson, 13 Nov. 1882; JWD, acc. 927, no. 47, ref. 38, Dawson to C. Tupper, 12 Feb. 1881.

67 JWD, acc. 927, no. 47, ref. 20, Dawson to T.H.S. White, 17 Feb. 1881; Spencer Baird to J.W. Dawson, 10 May, 17 May, 4 June 1883.

68 MC, acc. 1602, 1b, minute book (1882–92), 44, 48–9, 95.

69 Goode, "Principles," 81.

70 *Report of the Peter Redpath Museum for the Year 1869*, 21; ibid., 1897, 24; ibid., 1898, 38; MC, corporation minutes, 1894–1901, 398, 451; acc. 1459, 1, minute book (1892–1917), 82, 84; *Report of the Peter Redpath Museum for the Year 1899–1900*, 30.

71 José M. Gallardo, *El Museo de Ciencias Naturales en la Manzana de las Luces* (Buenos Aires: Imprenta Coni SACIFI 1976), 7–8; "Sumario sobre la fundacion y los progresos del Museo Público de Buenos Aires," *Anales del Museo Público de Buenos Aires* 1 (1864): 2–3, 7–9. For two conflicting views of the value of the museum collections see Thomas J. Hutchinson, *Buenos Aires and Argentine Gleanings* (London: E. Stanford 1865), 14, and Ernest William White, *Cameos from the Silver-land; or the Experiences of a Young Naturalist in the Argentine Republic*, 2 vols. (London: Van Voorst 1881–2), 1 : 196–8.

72 Horacio H. Camacho, "La Enseñanza y los estudios de las ciencias naturales," unpub. ms. in possession of the late José Babini, 10; Gallardo, *Museo de Ciencias*, 8.

73 Antonio Lascano González, *El Museo de Ciencias Naturales de Buenos Aires: Su Historia* (Buenos Aires: Ediciones Culturales Argentinas 1980), 87, 91; Max Biraben, *German Burmeister: Su vida, Su obra* (Buenos Aires: Ediciones Culturales Argentinas 1968), 31; M. Doello-Jurado, ed., *Memoria Anual de 1924* (Buenos Aires: Museo Nacional de Historia Natural "Bernardino Rivadavia" 1925) 93–4.

74 BAM, file M, no. 407, Burmeister to (unidentified) minister, 16 Sept. 1873.

75 Ibid., 1862; ibid., no. 418, "Cuenta de los gastos y entrados del Museo Público en el año 1873."

76 Ibid., no. 387, "Gastos del Museo Público en el año 1872."

77 Ibid., no. 656, Burmeister to Carlos D'Amico, 22 Jan. 1883.

78 Ibid., no. 790, Burmeister to Ministerio de Instrucción Pública, 8 Jan. 1885.

79 W.J. Holland, *To the River Plate and Back* (New York and London: Knickerbocker Press 1913), 246–7; BAM, file M, no. 486, Burmeister to Ministerio

de Gobierno, 10 July 1876; no. 653, Burmeister to Carlos D'Amico, 25 Jan. 1883.

80 Emile Daireaux, *Buenos-Ayres: La Pampa et la Patagonie* (Paris: Hachette 1877), 82–93.

81 Universidad Nacional de La Plata, *Obra del Centenario del Museo de La Plata* (La Plata: Facultad de Ciencias Naturales y Museo 1977), 1 (*Reseña Historica*): 36, 15–16, 8, 11, 60, 18.

82 Holland, *River Plate*, 115–19.

83 Ibid., 5, 75.

84 F. Moreno, "Breve Reseña de los progresos del Museo La Plata, durante el segundo semestre de 1888," *Boletin del Museo La Plata* (1889): 19; F. Moreno, "Museo La Plata: Informe Preliminar," *Boletin del Museo La Plata* (1888): 4, 24.

85 *Natural Science* 4 (1894): 1–21.

86 MCZ, H.A. Ward to Alexander Agassiz, 26 July 1889 (bAg879.10.1).

87 TL, folder 63, Flower to Haast, 20 Oct. 1873; HAW, Haast to H.A. Ward, 7 July 1881.

88 See for example Herbert M. Hale, "The First Hundred Years of the Museum: 1856–1956," *Records of the South Australian Museum* 12 (1956): 23.

CHAPTER FIVE

1 G.B. Goode, "The Principles of Museum Administration," Museums Association, *Report of Proceedings ... 1895 ... in Newcastle* (London: Museums Association 1895), 141.

2 Jeffrey Richards and John M. Mackenzie, *The Railway Station: A Social History* (Oxford: Oxford University Press 1986), 32.

3 On increased exchanges of specimens and advice see TL, folder 44, Haast correspondence with Cheeseman; folder 117, McCoy; and folder 142, Trimen. Kohlstedt also notes that intercolonial exchanges became more extensive in the 1880s. See Sally Gregory Kohlstedt, "Australian Museums of Natural History: Public Priorities and Scientific Initiatives in the 19th Century," *Historical Records of Australian Science* 6 (1983): 1–29, 104n.

4 Ronald Strahan, *Rare and Curious Specimens: An Illustrated History of the Australian Museum, 1827–1979* (Sydney: Australian Museum 1979), 18.

5 Herbert M. Hale, "The First Hundred Years of the Museum: 1856–1956," *Records of the South Australian Museum* 12 (1956): 19–20, 22–3. Roy MacLeod terms this new period of intercolonial cooperation in the late 1880s "federative science." See his "On Visiting the 'Moving Metropolis': Reflections on the Architecture of Imperial Science," *Historical Records of Australian Science* 5 (1982): 11–12.

6 For example, the South Australian Museum used statistics from the National Museum of Victoria; see Hale, "First Hundred Years," 27–8. As

mentioned in earlier chapters, Burmeister compared his staff with that of museums in Rio de Janeiro and La Plata; McCoy contrasted his appropriations with those of the Australian Museum in Sydney.

7 TL, folder 142, Trimen to Haast, 5 May 1873.

8 TL, folder 108, F.W. Hutton to Haast, 6 July 1874.

9 For example, see HAW, Cheeseman to Ward, 1 March 1886.

10 For example, see Hale, "First Hundred Years," 23; TL, folder 108, Hutton/ Haast correspondence; Sally Gregory Kohlstedt, "Natural Heritage: Securing Australian Materials in 19th Century Museums," *Museums Australia* (1984): 15–32; Sally Gregory Kohlstedt, "Historical Records in Australian Museums of Natural History," *Australian Historical Bibliography* 10 (1984): 73–4.

11 TL, folder 283, newspaper clipping dated 1884.

12 A.B. Meyer, *Studies of the Museums and Kindred Institutions of New York City, Albany, Buffalo, and Chicago, with Notes on Some European Institutions* (Washington, DC: Government Printing Office 1905), 521, 330; Anton Fritsch, "The Natural History Departments of the Bohemian Museum," *Natural Science* 8 (1896): 171.

13 Around this time, the British Museum's zoology department alone counted about 1.5 million specimens. See A.E. Gunther, *A Century of Zoology at the British Museum Through the Lives of Two Keepers, 1815–1914* (London: Dawsons 1975), 148. This view is supported by Markham and Oliver's 1933 survey; they found moderately-sized colonial cities and towns to be better endowed than their analogues in England. See S.F. Markham and W.R.B. Oliver, *A Report on the Museums and Art Galleries of New Zealand* (London: Museums Association 1933), 69.

14 *Report of the Peter Redpath Museum for the Year 1897*, 24.

15 W.J. Gardner, ed., *A History of Canterbury*, 2 vols. (Christchurch: Whitcombe & Tombs 1971), 2:235–6.

16 George Basalla, "The Spread of Western Science," *Science* 156 (1967): 617.

17 The Constitutional Act of 1852 created provinces under the jurisdiction of one colonial legislature. CM, Canterbury Provincial Secretary for Public Works, inwards letters, no. 220, Haast to Jollie, 22 Feb. 1869.

18 Hale, "First Hundred Years," 31. Aquiles D. Ygobone, *Francisco P. Moreno: Arquetipo de argentinidad* (Buenos Aires: Orientacion Cultural Editores 1953), 253.

19 TL, folder 110, Haast to Hutton, fragment, n.d.

20 Ann Moyal portrays McCoy as the most successful architect of museums in Australia; see A. Moyal, *"A Bright and Savage Land": Scientists in Colonial Australia* (Sydney: Collins 1986), 94–5; NMV, letterbook 3, 237, McCoy to Walker, 24 April 1868.

21 As, for example, occurred in 1875 when the provincial system ended in New Zealand; see Alan Lindsey McLeod, ed., *The Pattern of New Zealand Culture*

(Ithaca, NY: Cornell University Press 1968), 136.

22 Cyril Fox, *A Survey of McGill University Museums* (Montreal: McGill University Press, 1932), 4; A.H. McLintock, ed., *An Encyclopedia of New Zealand* 1:893.

23 Edward P. Alexander, *Museum Masters: Their Museums and Their Influence* (Nashville: American Association for State and Local History 1983), 16.

24 Sophie Forgan makes this point about the "functional adaptation" of different types of science buildings. See S. Forgan, "Context, Image, and Function: A Preliminary Enquiry Into the Architecture of Scientific Societies," *British Journal for the History of Science* 19 (1986): 91.

25 Anton Fritsch concurs with this view in his "The Museum Question in Europe and America," *Museums Journal* 3 (1904): 247. See also W. Boyd Dawkins, "On Museum Organisation and Arrangement," Museums Association, *Report of Proceedings ... 1890 ... at Liverpool* (London: Museums Association 1890), 38.

26 *Guide to the Collections in the Canterbury Museum*, 3d ed. (Christchurch: T.E. Fraser 1906), 2; F.A. Bather, "Some Colonial Museums," Museums Association, *Report of Proceedings ... 1894 ... in Dublin* (London: Museums Association 1895), 204.

27 Fritsch, "Museum Question," 248, 252–3. G. Brown Goode, "On the Classification of Museums," *Science*, n.s. 3 (1896): 159. Oliver Cummings Farrington also concludes that museums should first and foremost represent their own district; see O.C. Farrington, "Notes on European Museums," *The American Naturalist* 33 (1899): 780.

28 Henry H. Howorth, "Some Casual Thoughts on Museums," *Natural Science* 7 (1895): 97–100.

29 TL, folder 142, Trimen to Haast, 7 April 1879.

30 Hale, "First Hundred Years," 83. Kohlstedt ("Australian Museums," 15) notes that in the 1880s, local materials became "a point of pride and growing expertise."

31 Kenneth Hudson, *A Social History of Museums: What the Visitors Thought* (London: Macmillan & Co. 1975), 13, 69.

32 A.E. Parr, "On the Functions of the Natural History Museum," *Transactions of the New York Academy of Sciences* n.s. 2 (1939): 45.

33 This reorganization established the La Plata Museum as part of the faculty of natural sciences with professors at the head of each of the five sections of the museum (geology, biology, anthropology, geography, and chemistry). See Luis Maria Torres, ed., *Guía para Visitar el Museo de La Plata* (La Plata: República Argentina 1927), 10.

34 H.F. von Haast, *The Life and Times of Sir Julius von Haast* (Wellington: Avery Press 1948), 603, 609. Kohlstedt also describes how ties between universities and museums in Australia were tightened during this time ("Australian Museums," 16).

35 Both biologists and anthropologists suggest that the research function of museums had atrophied by the twentieth century; specimens are inadequate, inaccessible, neglected, and rarely consulted. See E.H. Miller, ed., *Museum Collections: Their Roles and Future ... in Biological Research*, occasional papers of the BC Provincial Museum no. 25 (British Columbia: BC Provincial Museum 1985), v; and George W. Stocking, ed., *Objects and Others: Essays on Museums and Material Culture* (Madison: University of Wisconsin Press 1985), 9.

36 L.V. Coleman, *The Museum in America*, 3 vols. (Washington, DC: American Association of Museums 1939), 3:225–6. For interesting insights into why museums were "on the defensive" by the twentieth century, see Parr, "Functions."

A Note on Sources

GENERAL SURVEYS AND HISTORIES
OF NATURAL HISTORY MUSEUMS

The best general treatment of the development of natural history museums is David Murray's two-volume *Museums: Their History and Their Use* (Glasgow: James MacLehose & Sons 1904). This work contains a superb bibliography organized according to subject. A special issue of UNESCO's *Journal of World History*, (14 [1972]) devoted to museums, provides a more recent survey. Kenneth Hudson's *Social History of Museums: What the Visitors Thought* (London: Macmillan & Co. 1975) provides a critical assessment of these developments; see also his *Museums of Influence* (Cambridge: Cambridge University Press 1987). The "Papers Presented at the International Conference on the History of Museums and Collections in Natural History," *Journal of the Society for the Bibliography of Natural History* 9 (1980): 365–670, explore a variety of issues related to particular museums.

A number of nineteenth-century naturalists tried to classify the profusion of institutions that flourished in their day. For a taxonomy suitable to the mid-century, see William Swainson "On the Formation and Arrangement of Collections" in his *Taxidermy, Bibliography, and Biography* (London: Longman 1840), 71–97. Somewhat later attempts include George Brown Goode's "On the Classification of Museums," *Science*, n.s. 3 (1896): 154–61, and A.C.L. Guenther's "Objects and Uses of Museums," *Report of the 50th Meeting of the British Association for the Advancement of Science; held at Swansea* (London: John Murray 1880), 591–8.

Discussion of the new museum idea stimulated an enormous literature on the proper arrangement of collections. J.E. Gray's views on the subject, presented in "Museums, Their Use and Improvement," *Report of*

*the 34th Meeting of the British Association for the Advancement of Science;
held at Bath* (London: John Murray 1865), 75–86, were further developed
and disseminated by William Henry Flower in his *Essays on Museums and
Other Subjects Connected With Natural History* (London: Macmillan & Co.
1889). The opposing view appears in Richard Owen's *On the Extent and
Aims of a National Museum of Natural History* (London: Saunders, Otley
& Co. 1862).

One line of debate, particularly concerned with the role of museums
as popular educators, includes A.R. Wallace's "Museums for the
People," *MacMillan's Magazine* 19 (1869): 244–50; W.A. Herdman, "An
Ideal Natural History Museum," *Proceedings of the Literary and Philosophical Society of Liverpool* 12 (1887): 61–81; W. Boyd Dawkins, "On Museum
Organisation and Arrangement," Museums Association, *Report of Proceedings ... 1890 ... at Liverpool* (London: Museums Association 1890),
38–45; R.H. Traquair, "President's Address," *Proceedings of the Royal
Physical Society* 121 (1891): 173–91; and W. Stanley Jevons, "The Use and
Abuse of Museums," in his *Methods of Social Reform* (London: Macmillan & Co. 1883), 53–81. Another part of the discussion centres upon the
idea of reorienting museums to serve the needs of a particular locality
above other considerations. See, for example, Henry H. Howorth,
"Some Casual Thoughts on Museums," *Natural Science* 7 (1895): 97–100,
and Anton Fritsch, "The Museum Question in Europe and America,"
Museums Journal 3 (1904): 247–56.

METROPOLITAN MUSEUMS

A large and growing literature treats natural history museums in Great
Britain, Europe, and the United States. For the first case, the already
great amount of attention paid to the British Museum has been further
increased by the publications issued to commemorate the centenary of
the opening of the Natural History Museum at South Kensington. See
J. Mordaunt Crook, *The British Museum* (London: Allen Lane 1972);
William T. Stearn, *The Natural History Museum at South Kensington* (Lon-
don: Heinemann 1981). A more popular account is Peter Whitehead and
Colin Keates's *The British Museum (Natural History)* (London: Philip
Wilson 1981). Mark Girouard presents a fascinating architectural history
in *Alfred Waterhouse and the Natural History Museum* (London: British
Museum 1981). A.E. Gunther's earlier *A Century of Zoology at the British
Museum Through the Lives of Two Keepers, 1815–1914* (London: Dawsons
1975) is in fact more useful than his more celebratory *Founders of Science
at the British Museum, 1753–1900* (Suffolk: Halesworth Press 1980). Biographies of directors and curators contain important information on the

British Museum. See for example Richard Owen, *The Life of Richard Owen*, 2 vols. (London: John Murray 1895), and Richard Lydekker, *Sir William Flower* (London: J.M. Dent & Co. 1906).

Although the British Museum is also described there, the *American Naturalist*'s surveys of European museums are more interesting for their discussion of continental museums. See Edmund Otis Hovey, "Notes on Some European Museums," *American Naturalist* 32 (1898): 697–715, and Oliver Cummings Farrington, "Notes on European Museums," *American Naturalist* 33 (1899): 763–81. For exclusively continental museums see Anton Fritsch, "The Natural History Departments of the Bohemian Museum," *Natural Science* 8 (1896): 168–72. For Paris, see Jean Schopfer, "Natural History Museum at Paris," *Architectural Record* 10 (1900): 55–75; Paul Lemoine, "National Museum of Natural History," *Natural History Magazine* 5 (1935): 4–19; and Camille Limoges, "The development of the Muséum d'Histoire Naturelle of Paris, *c.* 1800–1914," in Robert Fox and George Weisz, eds., *The Organization of Science and Technology in France 1808–1914* (Paris: Maison des Sciences de l'Homme and Cambridge: Cambridge University Press 1980), 211–40. The provincial museums of France are discussed in Louis Roule, "Les musées régionaux d'histoire naturelle et leur rôle dans l'enseignement public," *Revue scientifique* 61 (1923): 129–36.

A complete inventory of natural history museums in the United States, with information on their holdings and staffs, appears in Frederick J.H. Merrill's "Natural History Museums of the United States and Canada," *New York State Museum Bulletin* 62 (1903): 3–233. General surveys of US museums appear in Valentine Ball, *Report on the Museums of America and Canada* (London: Science & Art Department 1884); A.B. Meyer, *Studies of the Museums and Kindred Institutions of New York City, Albany, Buffalo, and Chicago, with Notes on Some European Institutions* (Washington, DC: Government Printing Office 1905); and Laurence Vail Coleman, *The Museum in America*, 3 vols. (Washington, DC: American Association of Museums 1939). The third volume of Coleman's work lists museums according to their area of specialization and means of support. An appendix organizes them by date of foundation.

Individual museums are treated by George N. Pindar, "The American Museum of Natural History: Its History and Expeditions," and Alexander Wetmore, "The Smithsonian Institution," both in Ludolph Brauer, ed., *Forschungsinstitute: ihre Geschichte, Organisation und Ziele*, 2 vols. (Hamburg: P. Hartung 1930), 2: 523–35 and 536–40. A more recent study of the American Museum is Geoffrey T. Hellman's *Bankers, Bones and Beetles: The First Century of the American Museum of Natural History* (Garden City, New York: Natural History Press, 1969).

National Museum, see G.B. Goode, ed., *The Smithsonian Institution;*
1846–1896. The History of Its First Half Century (Washington, DC:
De Vinne Press 1897), 303–66, and the short historical sketch in Philip
Kopper's lavishly illustrated *National Museum of Natural History* (New
York: Abrams 1982). For a fascinating account of a proprietary museum,
see Charles Coleman Sellers, *Mr. Peale's Museum: Charles Willson Peale
and the First Popular Museum of Natural Science and Art* (New York: W.W.
Norton & Co. 1980).

Museums in the United States gained international renown for their
pioneering work with new museum techniques and methods of display.
See Frederic A. Lucas, *The Story of Museum Groups* (New York: American Museum of Natural History 1925); Frank M. Chapman, *The
Habitat Groups of North American Birds* (New York: American Museum
of Natural History n.d.); F.A. Lucas, "Museum Methods: The Exhibition of Fossil Vertebrates," *Science*, n.s. 3 (1896): 573–75; and G.B.
Goode, "Recent Advances in Museum Methods," *Report of the U.S.
National Museum for the year ending 30 June 1893* (Washington, DC: Government Printing Office 1895), 23–58.

NATURAL HISTORY DEALERS
AND COLLECTORS

The progressiveness of United States museums, in terms of techniques
of displaying and preserving specimens, was largely due to the presence
of curators who had trained at Henry Ward's Natural Science Establish-
ment in Rochester, New York. For this development, see Frederic A.
Lucas, *Fifty Years of Museum Work* (New York: American Museum of
Natural History 1933). A full-length biography of Ward, written by his
grandson, appears in Roswell Ward, *Henry A. Ward: Museum Builder to
America* (Rochester, NY: Rochester Historical Society Publications 1948).
Sally Kohlstedt explores Ward's work as a natural history dealer in
"Henry A. Ward: The Merchant Naturalist and American Museum
Development," *Journal of the Society for the Bibliography of Natural History*
9 (1980): 647–61. These secondary sources provide only a tantalizing hint
of the richness of the Ward papers, which are kept in the Special Collections department of the University of Rochester Library. A considerable
portion of Ward's correspondence still remains unindexed. Especially
interesting for my purposes were the diaries Ward kept during his travels
to South America.

For Great Britain, D.E. Allen discusses the rise of professional collectors in his *Naturalist in Britain: A Social History* (London: Allen Lane
1976), 186ff. For collectors, dealers, and the sale of natural history speci-

mens at auction, see J.M. Chalmers-Hunt, comp., *Natural History Auctions 1700–1972: a Register of Sales in the British Isles* (London: Sotheby, Parke Bernet 1976) and E.G. Allingham, *A Romance of the Rostrum* (London: H.F. & G. Witherby 1924). Advertisements in such popular natural history periodicals of the day as *Scientific Opinion*, the *Scientific Record*, the *Naturalist*, and *Scientific Summary* are invaluable for recreating the world of natural history dealing. Also see the correspondence of curators at major metropolitan museums, for example, the Museum of Comparative Zoology and the British Museum (Natural History).

COLONIAL MUSEUMS

F.A. Bather's "Some colonial museums," Museums Association, *Report of Proceedings ... 1894 ... in Dublin* (London: Museums Association 1895), 193–239, defines the category of colonial museums and maps this territory for the first time. A generation later, the Museums Association commissioned a series of reports to explore each situation in greater detail; see S.F. Markham and H. Hargreaves, *The Museums of India* (London: Museums Association 1936); Henry A. Miers and S.F. Markham, *A Report on the Museums and Art Galleries of British Africa* (Edinburgh: T. & A. Constable 1932); H.A. Miers and S.F. Markham, *Reports on the Museums of Ceylon, British Malaya, the West Indies, etc.* (London: Museums Association 1933). A recent case study is Roger F.H. Summers's *History of the South African Museum, 1825–1975* (Cape Town: A.A. Balkema 1975).

MUSEUMS IN CANADA

There are a few secondary sources that discuss Canadian museums. One nineteenth-century survey is Henry Ami's *Report on the State of the Principal Museums in Canada and Newfoundland* (London: British Association for the Advancement of Science 1897). Its promising title notwithstanding, B.E. Walker's "Canadian Surveys, Museums, and the Need for Increased Expenditure Thereon," *Proceedings of the Royal Canadian Institute*, n.s. 2 (1900): 75–89, devotes most of its attention to surveys and little to museums. Twentieth-century overviews include: H.A. Miers and S.F. Markham, *A Report on the Museums of Canada* (Edinburgh: T. & A. Constable 1932); Carle E. Guthe and Grace M. Guthe, *The Canadian Museum Movement* (Ottawa: Canadian Museums Association 1958); and Archie F. Key, *Beyond Four Walls: the Origins and Development of Canadian Museums* (Toronto: McClelland & Stewart 1973). The most recent addition to this literature is Lovat Dickson's history of the Royal Ontario Museum, *The Museum Makers: The Story of the Royal*

Ontario Museum (Toronto: Royal Ontario Museum 1986).

The National Museum of Canada, whose early history is closely inter-twined with that of the Peter Redpath Museum, is treated in F.J. Alcock, *A Century in the History of the Geological Survey of Canada* (Ottawa: E. Cloutier 1947); Morris Zaslow, *Reading the Rocks* (Toronto: Macmillan & Co. 1975); Harlan I. Smith, "Museum Work at the Capital of Canada," *Proceedings of the American Association of Museums* 7 (1913): 28–35; and W.H. Collins, *The National Museum of Canada* (*Museums Annual Report for 1926*) (Ottawa: King's Printer 1927). The most thorough dis-cussion appears in W.A. Waiser's exemplary "Canada on Display: towards a National Museum, 1881–1911," in Richard A. Jarrell and Arnold E. Roos, eds., *Critical Issues in the History of Canadian Science, Technology and Medicine* (Thornhill and Ottawa: HSTC Publications 1983).

Dawson described the first natural history cabinet at McGill in his "Notice of the Natural History Collections of the McGill University," *Canadian Naturalist and Geologist* 7 (1862): 221–3. He discusses his diverse activities at McGill, including the creation and development of the Red-path Museum, in his *Fifty Years of Work in Canada: Scientific and Educa-tional* (Edinburgh and London: Ballantyne, Hanson & Co. 1901). See also his *In Memoriam: Peter Redpath, Governor and Benefactor of McGill University* (Montreal: "Witness" Printing House 1894). More informa-tion on Dawson, McGill, and the Redpath Museum appears in Stanley B. Frost's history of McGill, *McGill University for the Advancement of Learning* (Montreal: McGill-Queen's University Press 1980), 1:1801–95. See also my "'Stones and Bones and Skeletons': The Origins and Development of the Peter Redpath Museum," *McGill Journal of Educa-tion* 17 (1982): 45–64, and my "Better Than a Travelling Circus: Museums and Meetings in Montreal During the Early 1880s," *Transac-tions of the Royal Society of Canada* 4th ser. 20 (1982): 599–618. For an account of the state of the museum fifty years after its foundation, see Cyril Fox's *Survey of McGill University Museums* (Montreal: McGill Uni-versity 1932), which was produced as part of the Miers and Markham survey.

The early history of the Peter Redpath Museum may be drawn from materials held in the McGill University Archives. These include two minute books covering the years 1882–92 and 1892–1917, which record the meetings of the Redpath Museum Committee. The archives has also kept a complete series of annual reports of the museum; these may be introduced by the information contained in the *Guide to Visitors to the Peter Redpath Museum of McGill University* (Montreal: 1885). These hold-ings pertain to the Redpath Museum exclusively, but supplementary material exists in the papers of J.W. Dawson. These contain much cor-respondence relevant to the museum's development.

MUSEUMS IN NEW ZEALAND

The only comprehensive study of museums in New Zealand is S.F. Markham and W.R.B. Oliver, *A Report on the Museums and Art Galleries of New Zealand* (London: Museums Association 1933). Also see the comments in "New Zealand Museums," *Museums Journal* 1 (1901–2): 200–1.

Much of the history of the Canterbury Museum can be reconstructed from the biography of Julius Haast by his son, H.F. von Haast, *The Life and Times of Sir Julius von Haast* (Wellington: Avery Press 1948). See also *Guide to the Collections in the Canterbury Museum* 3d ed. (Christchurch: T.E. Fraser 1906); S.H. Jenkinson, *New Zealanders and Science* (Wellington: Department of Internal Affairs 1940), ch. 4; and Peggy Burton, *The New Zealand Geological Survey, 1865–1965* (Wellington: New Zealand Department of Scientific and Industrial Research 1965), 10–16. Archival sources, however, remain invaluable. In New Zealand, these include the fragmentary records held by the Canterbury Museum: incoming letters of the Canterbury provincial Secretary for Public Works; a file of Haast correspondence; and a box of reports of the Canterbury Provincial Council, which are succeeded by the Annual Reports of the Canterbury Museum. The Canterbury Public Library holds another folder of museum records from 1869 to 1874; this is a copy of an official file from the Canterbury Provincial Government Archives. The library also has some Haast correspondence and the journal of the Canterbury Provincial Council. Especially valuable are the Haast papers in the Alexander Turnbull Library in Wellington, New Zealand. File MS 37 is the major repository of Haast's correspondence and also contains notebooks and newspaper clippings concerning the Canterbury Museum. A large number of Haast letters are indexed in the Ward papers in Rochester, New York. Haast's correspondence with Richard Owen is held by the British Museum (Natural History). The Museum of Comparative Zoology has Haast's correspondence with Alexander Agassiz and other figures.

AUSTRALIAN MUSEUMS

After Bather, the first general survey of Australian museums is S.F. Markham and H.C. Richards, *A Report on the Museums and Art Galleries of Australia* (London: Museums Association 1933). Recently Sally Gregory Kohlstedt has reached new levels of sophistication and interpretation in her "Australian Museums of Natural History: Public Priorities and Scientific Initiatives in the Nineteenth Century," *Historical Records of Australian Science* 6 (1983): 1–29.

Individual Australian museums also have been studied. For the South

Australian Museum in Adelaide, see Herbert M. Hale, "The First Hundred Years of the Museum, 1856–1956," *Records of the South Australian Museum* 12 (1956). On the Australian Museum in Sydney, see Ronald Strahan, *Rare and Curious Specimens: An Illustrated History of the Australian Museum, 1827–1979* (Sydney: Australian Museum 1979). On the Queensland Museum, see Patricia Mather et al., *A Time for a Museum: The History of the Queensland Museum, 1862–1986* (South Brisbane: Queensland Museum 1986).

For Melbourne, R.T.M. Pescott's *Collections of a Century: The History of the First Hundred Years of the National Museum of Victoria* (Melbourne: National Museum of Victoria 1954) is invaluable. Information on McCoy and the National Museum also appears in Geoffrey Blainey, *A Centenary History of the University of Melbourne* (Melbourne: Melbourne University Press 1957), and Ernest Scott, *A History of the University of Melbourne* (Melbourne: Melbourne University Press 1936).

The archives of the National Museum of Victoria are the most voluminous and best organized for any of the museums studied here. All is readily put at the disposal of the researcher. The archives' holdings include an invoice book; four letterbooks covering the years 1857–61, 1861–5, 1865–73, and 1873–8; and an account book of the agents general for crown colonies. The letterbooks contain the returns of the National Museum for the years 1861 through 1869; these are continued by the annual *Reports ... of the Public Library, Museums, and National Gallery of Victoria*. Other important correspondence appears in various boxes labelled with names of foreign museums, dealers, and collectors. The Mitchell Library in Sydney also holds a reel of microfilm which contains a volume of McCoy correspondence (CY 499). These letters treat McCoy's early years in Australia and particularly his close relationship with Adam Sedgwick. In England, letters from McCoy are contained in the Owen correspondence at the British Museum (Natural History), vol. 18, as well as in the Sedgwick correspondence in the Manuscripts Reading Room of the Cambridge University Library.

For McCoy's personal views on the place and functions of museums, see his extremely rare *On the Formation of Museums in Victoria* (Melbourne: Goodhugh & Hough 1857). The Philosophical Institute of Victoria declined to publish this address of 15 July 1856 in its *Transactions*. For McCoy's quarrels with W.B. Clarke, see Ann Mozley Moyal, *Scientists in Nineteenth Century Australia: A Documentary History* (Melbourne: Cassell Australia 1976); T.G. Vallance, "The Fuss About Coal: Troubled Relations Between Palaebotany and Geology" D.F. and S.G.M. Carr, eds. *Plants and Man in Australia* (Sydney: Academic Press 1981), 136–76, esp. 148ff.; and Elena Grainger, *The Remarkable Reverend Clarke* (Melbourne: Oxford University Press 1982), esp. 220–5.

MUSEUMS IN SOUTH AMERICA

The only general survey of museums on this continent is Laurence Vail Coleman, *Directory of Museums in South America* (Washington, DC: American Museums Association 1929). For the early history of the Buenos Aires Museum, see Angel J. Carranza, "Anales del Museo Público de Buenos Aires," *Revista de Buenos Aires* 8 (1865): 273–83, 442–6, 612–17 and Eduardo L. Holmberg, "El Museo de Buenos Aires," *El Naturalista Argentino* 1 (1878): 33–43. For Burmeister's own account, see the "Proemio" and "Sumario sobre la fundacion y los progresos del Museo Público de Buenos Aires," *Anales del Museo Público de Buenos Aires* 1 (1864): iii–iv and 1–11. See also the "Proemio," *Anales del Museo Público de Buenos Aires* 2 (1870–4): iv. Still more information is contained in Burmeister's "Observations on the Various Species of *Glyptodon* in the Public Museum of Buenos Aires," *Annals and Magazine of Natural History* 3d ser. 14 (1864): 81–97.

Twentieth-century accounts include one by the present director of the museum, José M. Gallardo, *El Museo de Ciencias Naturales en la Manzana de las Luces* (Buenos Aires: Imprenta Coni SACIFI 1976). See also the more recent quasi-official history of the museum by Antonio Lascano González, *El Museo de Ciencias Naturales de Buenos Aires: Su Historia* (Buenos Aires: Ediciones Culturales Argentinas 1980). On the University of Buenos Aires, which has always enjoyed a close relationship with the Buenos Aires museum, see Horacio H. Camacho, "La Enseñaza y los estudios de las ciencias naturales," unpub. ms., in possession of the late José Babini, and Camacho's *Las Ciencias Naturales en la Universidad de Buenos Aires* (Buenos Aires: Editorial Universitaria de Buenos Aires 1971).

The archives of the Buenos Aires Museum nevertheless remain indispensable for recreating the early history of the institution. I was given access to the Correspondencia de Oficio del Director del Museo Público de Buenos Aires, 1862–92, organized according to year. These annual files are further divided alphabetically. Their contents include annual budgets of the museum and Burmeister's correspondence with various figures, particularly government ministers. The only other Burmeister papers that I have located that relate to his activities as a museum builder are his letters to Spencer Baird in the archives of the Smithsonian Institution.

For short biographies of the various figures involved with the history of museums in greater Buenos Aires, see Max Biraben, "Ciento Cincuenta Años de Zoología Argentina," *Physis* 22, no. 63 (1961): 1–20. Florentino Ameghino plays a role in the development of the Buenos Aires Museum, and, more importantly, in that of the La Plata Museum.

See Ameghino's *Obras Completas y correspondencia científica de Florentino Ameghino*, ed. Alfredo J. Torcelli, 24 vols. (La Plata: Taller de impresiones oficiales 1935), esp. vols. 20 and 21; and Fernando Márquez Miranda, *Ameghino: une Vida Heroica* (Buenos Aires: Editorial Nova 1951). On Burmeister, see Max Biraben, *German Burmeister: su vida, su obra* (Buenos Aires: Ediciones Culturales Argentinas 1968); for Moreno, see Aquiles D. Ygobone, *Francisco P. Moreno: Arquetipo de Argentinidad* (Buenos Aires: Orientacion Cultural Editores 1953) and José Liebermann, "Francisco P. Moreno, Precursor Argentino," *Anales de la Sociedad Científica Argentina* 140 (1945): 396–427.

The most detailed account of the history of the La Plata Museum appears in Universidad Nacional de La Plata, *Obra del Centenario del Museo de La Plata* (La Plata: Facultad de Ciencias Naturales y Museo 1977), 1 (*Reseña Histórica*). Also see Luis María Torres, ed., *Guía para Visitar el Museo de La Plata* (La Plata: República Argentina 1927). Moreno's progress reports appear in the *Boletin del Museo La Plata*: "Museo La Plata: Informe Preliminar," (1888): 3–35, and "Breve Reseña de los progresos del Museo La Plata, durante el segundo semestre de 1888," (1889): 5–44. The University of La Plata was closely associated with the development of the museum; see Benito A. Nazar Anchorena, *La Universidad Nacional de La Plata en el año 1926* (Buenos Aires: J. Peuser 1927), esp. 95–127. Archives describing the creation and early development of the museum unfortunately have not been kept at La Plata. The only correspondence of Moreno that I have been able to locate is held in the archives of the Smithsonian Institution.

Index